FINALLY, A DICTIONARY JUST FOR HUE

Have you ever been *green with envy*? *Yellow bellied*? *Blackballed*? Or perhaps you've just had a case of the *blues*. If you have, you've probably noticed that the English language is filled with hundreds of clichés and terms that employ color imagery. This fascinating book takes an in-depth yet lighthearted look at the etymologies of this wonderful rainbow of colorful colloquialisms that enrich our language and allow us to convey our thoughts with vividness and clarity. In sections devoted to each color family, *Seeing Red or Tickled Pink* explores the derivations of these phrases, explaining how each was first used and how their meanings have evolved over time. You'll find out why a *blue funk* is likely to result in a *white knight* followed by a *black day*. You'll learn how *yellow journalism* got its name (which has nothing to do with cowardly reporters), and why calling someone a *bluestocking* is a sexist remark. As far as reference books go, this one is a *horse of a different color*— a useful tool for writers and teachers, a delightful diversion for students, and perfect gift for the word-lover in your life.

CHRISTINE AMMER, an acclaimed lexicographer, is the author of more than a dozen reference books, including four volumes on language: *Southpaws & Sunday Punches and Other Sporting Expressions*; *It's Raining Cats and Dogs and Other Beastly Expressions*; *Fighting Words from War, Rebellion, and Other Combative Capers*; and *Have a Nice Day—No Problem! A Dictionary of Clichés* (also available from Plume). A graduate of Swarthmore College, she lives in Lexington, Massachusetts.

OTHER BOOKS BY CHRISTINE AMMER

Have a Nice Day—No Problem! A Dictionary of Clichés

*It's Raining Cats and Dogs and
Other Beastly Expressions*

*Fighting Words from War, Rebellion and Other
Combative Capers*

Getting Help: A Consumer's Guide to Therapy

The New A to Z of Women's Health

The HarperCollins Dictionary of Music

Unsung: A History of Women in American Music

The A to Z of Investing

Christine Ammer

Seeing Red or Tickled Pink

Color Terms in Everyday Language

A PLUME BOOK

PLUME
Published by the Penguin Group
Penguin Books USA Inc., 375 Hudson Street,
New York, New York 10014, U.S.A.
Penguin Books Ltd, 27 Wrights Lane, London W8 5TZ, England
Penguin Books Australia Ltd, Ringwood, Victoria, Australia
Penguin Books Canada Ltd, 10 Alcorn Avenue,
Toronto, Ontario, Canada M4V 3B2
Penguin Books (N.Z.) Ltd, 182–190 Wairau Road,
Auckland 10, New Zealand

Penguin Books Ltd, Registered Offices:
Harmondsworth, Middlesex, England

Published by Plume, an imprint of New American Library,
a division of Penguin Books USA Inc.
Previously published in a Dutton edition.

First Plume Printing, November, 1993
10 9 8 7 6 5 4 3 2 1

 REGISTERED TRADEMARK—MARCA REGISTRADA

LIBRARY OF CONGRESS CATALOGING-IN-PUBLICATION DATA
Ammer, Christine.
    Seeing red or tickled pink : color terms in everyday language /
Christine Ammer.
        p.   cm.
    Includes index.
    ISBN 0-452-27040-5
    1. English language—Terms and phrases.   2. English language—
Etymology.   3. Colors, Words for.   4. Figures of speech.
I. Title.
[PE1689.A49   1993]
422—dc20   93–8209
                                                                 CIP

Printed in the United States of America

Contents

ɞ ɞ ɞ ɞ ɞ ɞ ɞ ɞ ɞ

Preface

ɞ ɞ ɞ ɞ ɞ ɞ ɞ ɞ ɞ

*J*ust as color adds a vital dimension to the visual world, so the idioms involving color have enhanced our language. Without them we would in effect be speaking in *black and white*, and we would be much the poorer for it.

The 750 or so terms in this book are arranged into twelve general categories: colors, black, blue, brown, gray, green, orange, pink (and rose), purple (and violet), red, white, and yellow. The order of these categories could have followed the order of the spectrum, or that of primary and secondary colors, or some other way. Instead, it is, except for the first, alphabetical. Within each chapter, the order is at best arbitrary. For seeking out any particular term or group of terms, the reader is advised to consult the complete index at the back of the book.

Cross-references are indicated in small capital letters, for example, see BLACKAMOOR. Please consult the index for the precise page.

Abbreviations are confined to one, the *OED*, for *Oxford English Dictionary*, that masterpiece of etymology without which books like this could never be attempted. Citations from the Bible identify chapter and verse, and from plays, the act and scene, in the conventional fashion of 1:2, where 1 represents chapter (or act) and 2 is the verse (or scene).

The author is deeply indebted to a long line of eminent etymologists, linguists, and lexicographers who collectively represent centuries of work in tracing the origins of the English language. This book is a modest compilation of the results of a fraction of their scholarship. Grateful acknowledgment is also made to the many friends and acquaintances who have helped trace origins of elusive terms, track down song lyrics, and contribute arcane bits of information. Their assistance has greatly smoothed the way.

All the Colors of the Rainbow

A remarkable number of terms and phrases in our language refer to color. Some of them, such as *feeling blue, seeing red,* or *tickled pink,* associate colors with specific human emotions. Others, such as *blue blood, white cockade,* and *red carpet,* have honorable origins from the Middle Ages. And still others, among them *yellow journalism,* the *Red Guard,* and the *Black and Tans,* have an interesting although more recent history.

> *Blue is true, Yellow's jealous,*
> *Green's forsaken, Red's brazen,*
> *White is love. And Black is death.*
>
> —J. O. HALLIWELL,
> *Nursery Rhymes of England* (1842)

Practically every people and culture have used color symbolically—that is, assigned a variety of qualities and even specific objects to certain colors. According to *Funk & Wagnalls Standard Dictionary of Folklore*, in Western art *blue* stands for constancy and truth; *green* for fruitfulness and hope; *orange* for benevolence, earthly wisdom, and fire; *purple* for love of truth, loyalty, martyrdom, and royalty; *red* for blood, love, patriotism, and valor; *white* for day, innocence, perfection, and purity; *yellow* for divinity and the highest values; *black* for death, despair, and evil; *brown* for barrenness and penitence; and *gray* for barrenness, death, and despair. Further, some of these same colors also have negative associations: green with envy, orange with the devil, purple with mourning.

The Roman Catholic Church has long used a different set of symbols: blue for humility and expiation; black and violet for grief as well as death; green for God's bounty, gladness, and the Resurrection; light green for baptism; red for martyrdom; and so on.

Not everyone held to these conventions. Thus Charles Kingsley wrote, in *Dartside* (1849):

Oh green is the colour of faith and truth,
And rose the colour of love and youth,
And brown of the fruitful clay.

Nor is such color symbolism confined to the West. To the Pueblo Indians each color meant a particular direction: white is east; yellow (or blue or black) west; blue (or yellow) south; etc. The precise assignment of color varied with each tribe. The Cherokee Indians, on the other hand, associated both directions and abstract qualities with color: red with east and success; blue, north and trouble; black, west and death; and white, south and happiness.

🕭 *All the Colors of the Rainbow* 🕭

A flower de luse . . . hath all the colours of a
Rainebowe.

—G. LEGH, *Accidence of Armoury* (1562)

The rainbow is one of nature's most colorful phenomena. This arc of prismatic color, which today we know is caused by the refraction and reflection of the sun's rays in drops of rain, consists of the seven colors of the spectrum: red, orange, yellow, green, blue, indigo, and violet.

The rainbow was a source of wonder to primitive and ancient peoples the world over. The ancient Greeks regarded it with dismay. In Homer's *Iliad* (c. 850 B.C.) Zeus, the god of gods, stretches forth a lurid rainbow to be a portent of evil. But the ancient Hebrews viewed it quite differently: "I do set my bow in the cloud, and it shall be for a token of a covenant between me and the earth," God told Noah, assuring him there would not be another great flood (Genesis 9:13).

In myth the rainbow was the bow a sky deity used to fight against storm demons, as well as a bridge between heaven and earth. In folklore it was a symbol of the divine presence and therefore of hope, peace, resurrection, and victory. Christian philosophers of the Middle Ages likened its seven rays to the seven gifts of the Holy Spirit —the fourfold nature of man's perfection (in body, mind, soul, and spirit) and the threefold nature of the Trinity (Father, Son, and Holy Ghost).

Not unreasonably the rainbow also has figured in weather forecasting. According to Leonard Digges, a rainbow in the morning was a sign that bad weather was coming, whereas a rainbow in the evening was a sign of good weather (*Prognostication*, c. 1555).

And, of course, rainbows have always appealed to

poets, from Shakespeare, who said that adding another hue to the rainbow is "ridiculous excess," to the lyricists of such popular songs as "Over the Rainbow" (E. Y. Harburg, 1938) and "I'm Always Chasing Rainbows" (Joseph McCarthy, 1918). The latter refers to the old myth that a pot of gold is buried under the place where a rainbow touches the earth. Reaching this spot is, of course, impossible, giving rise to the term *rainbow chasers* for those who pursue or hope for the impossible.

🍂 *Clashing Colors* 🍂

All colours will agree in the dark.

—FRANCIS BACON, *Essays* (1625)

Certain colors are said to "go together," and others are said to "clash." Exactly which sets of colors do so is a matter of artistic convention, and even of fashion. "Where tawdry Yellow strove with dirty Red," wrote Alexander Pope (*Moral Essays*, 1735). Half a century ago redheads were told never to wear pink, fashion decreeing that pink and red were an ill-suited combination. Today this dictum is frequently ignored, and pink and red are often seen in combination.

Colors more often clash in a figurative sense, in that they have long been used to differentiate opposing sides in competitions, ranging from warfare (see THE COLORS) to games and sports. Probably for this reason, many team names include a color: baseball's White Sox and Red Sox; football's Harvard Crimson and Yale Blue; crew's Oxford Blue and Cambridge Light Blue.

Black and white, which are considered colors even though they are not part of the spectrum, are similarly used to differentiate opposing sides. They operate in checkers and chess; in chess problems white always is "to move and win."

❧ *The Color Bar* ❧

He's really awfully fond of colored people. Well, he says himself, he wouldn't have white servants.

—DOROTHY PARKER,
Arrangement in Black and White

Black and white also are used as racial descriptions, despite the fact that the so-called white race is actually closer to pink-skinned, and the so-called black is various shades of brown. An early instance appears in an account of 1400 that describes Numidians as being "blakk of colour."

The separation of black and white, and the regard of the one as inferior by the other, long antedates Dorothy Parker's acerbic description of racial prejudice. In the nineteenth century the word *colored* came to be considered more polite than "black" or "Negro." In the most famous abolitionist writing of the century, the novel *Uncle Tom's Cabin* (1850), Harriet Beecher Stowe writes, "Among the colored circles of New Orleans." And the abolitionist poet John Greenleaf Whittier wrote of Haitian patriot Toussaint L'Ouverture, "Dark Haytien!—for the time shall come . . . when everywhere thy name shall be redeemed from color's infamy."

Long after the abolition of slavery in the United States, the *color bar* or *color line* separating black from white socially, economically, and politically survived. Although in 1878 the *North American Review* editorialized, "We shall soon cease to hear of a color-line," nearly a century later President John F. Kennedy still found it necessary to tell Congress, "There are no 'white' or 'colored' signs on the foxholes or graveyards of battle" (message to Congress urging the passage of the Civil Rights Act of 1963).

In South Africa "colored" has long had a different meaning—that is, people of mixed race. In America today, "colored" is heard somewhat less, and those with skin other than "white" are now being described as people *of color.* However, one of the oldest organizations of its kind in America, the National Association for the Advancement of Colored People (NAACP), founded in 1909, has retained its original name. (Also see BLACKAMOOR in the next chapter.)

ᴣ◕ *Color Blindness* ᴣ◕

I suffer from an incurable disease—color blindness.

—ARCHBISHOP JOOST DE BLANK

The statement above, attributed to this staunchly anti-apartheid South African clergyman, transfers this inborn physical disability to figurative blindness to racial differences. He was not the inventor of this figure of speech, which dates from the mid-nineteenth century. But the disability itself was first described only about 1794, by scientist John Dalton.

Dalton, who himself was afflicted with it, called the inability to see certain colors or to discriminate between individual shades of color "Daltonism." It was renamed *color blindness* by Sir David Brewster (1781–1868), the inventor of the kaleidoscope, and first appeared in print in *Diseases of the Eye* (1854), an ophthalmology text.

Color blindness, which would be more appropriately called defective color vision, is thought to be very common. It rarely consists of total inability to distinguish colors, but more often is the tendency to confuse colors. When such confusion involves the colors red and green, used to indicate "stop" and "go" in traffic lights, it can be hazardous (this form is sometimes called red-green color blindness). Usually, however, color blindness is more inconvenient than disabling.

❧ *Changing Color* ❧

> *When Michael saw this host, he first grew pale,*
> *As angels can; next, like Italian twilight,*
> *He turn'd all colours . . .*
>
> —GEORGE GORDON, LORD BYRON
> *The Vision of Judgment* (1822)

To *change color* has meant to turn pale since the late thirteenth century and to blush since the mid-fifteenth century. And eventually it acquired a third meaning, to regain one's color after turning pale.

In nature, changing color is a basic form of protection for some species and indeed is referred to as *protective coloring*. Prime among them is the chameleon, a lizard that can change both its color and its color pattern to make it blend with its surroundings and appear less conspicuous to its enemies. In humans, however, changing color has been identified with cowardice since 850 B.C., in Homer's *Iliad*. "The color of the brave man changeth not," he wrote, which was later quoted by Plutarch, and again, "The color of the coward changeth ever to another hue" (later quoted by Erasmus in his *Adagia*). It was still current in Shakespeare's time: "His coward lips did from their colour fly" (*Julius Caesar*, 1:2).

The Elizabethan age also saw another mode of changing color, the use of cosmetics. Thomas Dekker's poem *A Description of a Lady by Her Lover* (c. 1632) has it:

The reason why fond women love to buy
Adulterate complexion: here 'tis read.—
False colours last after the true be dead.

Changing colors can involve more than one kind of pretense. Indeed, *under color of* has meant under pretense or pretext since c. 1340, when Hampole's *Psalter* had: "Vndire colour of goed counsaile bryngis til syn" (Under color of good counsel persuades [someone] to sin). This term, however, means something quite different from being *under someone's colors* (see below).

🙟 *The Colors* 🙟

A *call to the colors, to stand by one's colors, to be under someone's colors*—the "colors" in these phrases all refer to an ensign or flag and, by extension, to the loyalty it commands. When Shakespeare described the exiled duke of Norfolk's death in *Richard II* (4:1):

And there at Venice gave
. . . his pure soul unto his captain Christ,
Under whose colours he had fought so long . . .

he indicated that the Duke died in combat while fighting for the Christian (Crusaders') side against the Turks and Saracens.

🙟 *Sailing Under False Colors* 🙟

Today, *to sail under false colors* means to deceive by pretending to be something one is not, or by behaving hypocritically. The term comes from the pirates' common trick of hanging out a friendly nation's flag to lure a vessel close enough so as to attack and board it. The expression was used figuratively by the sixteenth century or so. Sir Thomas Elyot had a version of it in *The Governour* (1531): "He wyll . . . sette a false colour of lernyng on proper wittes, which wyll be wasshed away with one shoure of raine." And in 1711 Richard Steele wrote in *The Spectator*, "Our Female Candidate . . . will no longer hang out false Colours." Obviously it was her views Steele was referring to, and not her makeup.

Someone sailing under false colors might well decide to *come out in her true colors*—that is, reveal her true character. This term is somewhat newer, perhaps because true is less appealing than false. In any event, it dates only from the late eighteenth century. Dickens had it in *The Old Curiosity Shop* (1840): "[He] who didn't venture . . . to come out in his true colours."

The old term *to nail one's colors to the mast* also has a maritime origin. A flag nailed to the mast cannot easily be hauled down. Hence this became a metaphor for an unyielding position or attitude. Dickens so used it in *Dombey and Son* (1848): "Mrs. Chick had nailed her colours to the mast."

Still current is *to come off with flying colors*, meaning to win or succeed. It refers to the practice of a victorious fleet flying flags from the masthead as it sails into port and has been used figuratively since the seventeenth century.

ა Colorful or Colorless? ა

Whether true or false, some color appears to be preferable to no color at all. The adjective *colorless* has been used figuratively to mean dull, or lacking a bright or distinctive character, from the mid-nineteenth century. Writing about William Pitt, for example, Archibald Primrose (1847–1929) talked of "the colorless photography of a printed record" compared to a live speech. In contrast, *colorful* has meant lively, full of force, interest, or excitement since the late nineteenth century, and much earlier than that color was figuratively equated with verve and brilliance. "To paint out that puisant Prince in such lively colours as hee deserveth," wrote Abraham Fleming (*A Panoplie of Epistles*, 1576).

Fleming's metaphor might be considered an early version of *living color*, a term invented by some imaginative copywriter for the National Broadcasting Company and its parent, RCA, to advertise their wonderful commercial innovation, color television shows and sets that could receive them. The term *color television* first made its way into print in 1929 in a book that said, "Baird was partially successful in color television in 1928" (Sheldon and Grisewood, *Television*). A related term, *colorcast*, for color television broadcast, appeared in the linguistics journal *American Speech* in 1949.

🍂 *A Coat of Many Colors* 🍂

Joseph is one of the most familiar figures from the Old Testament. He was the best-loved son of Rachel and Jacob, born to them in their old age, and consequently roused the jealousy of his older brothers. To show his fatherly love, Jacob "made him a coat of many colors" (Genesis 37:3). The Bible gives no further details about this garment except that it helped bring on misfortune, for, envious both of his position as a favorite and of his beautiful coat, his brothers sold Joseph into slavery. Eventually, of course, Joseph attained a position of power in Egypt, and during a subsequent famine he showed kindness to the brothers who had mistreated him.

🙶 *Artistic Color* 🙶

Color has been vital to painters since prehistoric times. The ancient cave paintings that survive used all kinds of odd substances to make their mark on stone. Artists are, not unnaturally, fussy about the colors in their surroundings as well as in their work, and try to arrange them to their liking.

The term *color scheme* refers to any planned arrangement of colors to please the eye. It came into use about the turn of the twentieth century and continues to be current, particularly among interior decorators and fashion designers. One of its early uses, however, was by a woman who was more of an "exterior" decorator, Britain's outstanding garden expert of her day, Gertrude Jekyll, who wrote the book *Colour Schemes for the Flower Garden* (1914).

Artists were the first to use the term *local color*, by which they meant realistic color—the color natural to

each object being painted. In the nineteenth century this term was transferred to literature and drama to describe the portrayal of vivid, characteristic details and peculiarities of a particular time and place.

For very young would-be artists, that great American entrepreneur Walt Disney began marketing his *Mickey Mouse Coloring Book* in 1931. Although it was probably not the first *coloring book*—a collection of outline drawings that are to be colored in with crayons, pencils, or some other medium—it did much to popularize this pastime. Schoolteachers sternly admonished those youngsters who failed to "color inside the lines," seen as evidence of sloppiness rather than a creative bent.

A related form of adult pastime is the *color by number* painting, an outline drawing that is numerically coded so the painter knows which color to fill in where.

Color coding today is used in a variety of enterprises, ranging from a method of indicating harmonies to be played on a guitar to marking electrical lead wires. It saves time and perhaps also eliminates error.

The ravished coloratura trilling madly off-key.

—W. H. AUDEN, *Sea and Mirror* (1944)

Coloratura is simply Italian for "coloring" or "colored." In the late seventeenth century it began to be used for vocal music that is ornamented with rapid runs, trills, cadenzas, and similar florid passagework. The *OED* cites the first reference in English to it in a 1740 translation of S. de Brossard's music dictionary, and it has been so used ever since, both for such music and for the kind of voice—light, flexible, and usually soprano—required to perform it.

A coloratura voice is distinguished from other kinds partly by its distinctive *tone color*, a term used to describe the particular quality of sound that differentiates the

same note played on a flute or clarinet, for example, or
sung by a soprano or contralto. Also called "timbre," tone
color is determined by the particular harmonics sounded
and their relative loudness. Combining different instruments, each with its own tone color, is an important consideration in musical composition, just as combining
colors is important in the visual arts.

ও *A Horse of a Different Color* ও

Exactly why *a horse of a different color* was originally
selected to represent "another matter entirely" is no
longer known. Some etymologists believe this saying was
first suggested by Shakespeare, who in *Twelfth Night*
(2:3) has "My purpose is indeed a horse of that colour."
The Bard, of course, meant "Yes, this is just what I in-
tend," whereas the current locution is negative (this is
different). More likely the modern term comes from the
racecourse, where, perhaps, an unsuccessful bettor decided to try again and rationalized his new choice with
this statement. In any event, the term has been used in
the United States since the late eighteenth century and
soon crossed the Atlantic to Britain. A correspondent of
lexicographer Richard H. Thornton's told him that his
grandfather, writing of James Polk's election to the Pres-
idency in 1844, said, "They thought he would never win,
but he proved a grey horse of a different color." (This
election, incidentally, is believed to be the source of the
expression "dark horse.")

Betting of one kind or another may also be the source
of *Let's see the color of your money*, meaning, first prove
that you can pay up before we go on. This slangy phrase
is a twentieth-century Americanism, according to Eric
Partridge, and crossed the Atlantic unchanged. Another
color term, however, may have quite different meanings,
depending on where it is uttered. To be *off-color* in Britain

means to be either ailing or a bit seedy. J. G. Holland used it thus in *Sevenoaks* (1875), "Everybody . . . considered her a little 'off color.' " In America, on the other hand, it means of doubtful propriety or dubious taste, a meaning later adopted in Britain as well. An *off-color joke*, for example, is decidedly risqué, or, more baldly put, a dirty joke; it is not to be repeated in decorous company. The *OED* cites an early use of this sense in the *National Police Gazette* in 1883, which refers to the "off-color morals" of the stage.

Black, Black, Black Is the Color . . .

*I*n a familiar American folk song, black is the color of "my true love's hair," but that is one of the relatively few favorable references to this color. The majority of idioms and allusions equate black with sinister, malignant, or deadly. Thus *black art* is the art of the devil. To *blackball* or *blackmail* someone is a long way from doing him a favor, and *black Monday* or a *black future* are scarcely events to look forward to.

Literally, black means absorbing all light, without reflecting any of its rays. By extension it means the absence of light, or darkness. Yet long before the physics of light was understood, the word black was in common use. In Old English it was *blaec*, closely related to its equivalents in Old High German (*blah, blach*) and Old Norse (*blakkr*). And even older than that, in many languages and cultures, was the association of black with evil (and white with good). "For all the sin wherewith the Face of Man is blacken'd," wrote Edward Fitzgerald in his translation of the twelfth-century Persian poet Omar Khayyám.

Both in art and in religion black signified sin, despair, and mourning. Indeed, its use in mourning is very old indeed; it probably comes from the ancient Semitic custom of blackening the face with dirt or ashes to make it unrecognizable to the malignant dead, as well as a mark of grief and submission. (In China, on the other hand, white is the color of mourning.) At Roman funerals mutes wore black garments, a custom that long persisted, although later mutes were replaced by ordinary servants. Beaumont and Fletcher refer to it in their play *Monsieur Thomas* (c. 1610):

> . . . *give me leave to live a little longer.*
> *You stand about me like my Blacks.*

Despite the color's many negative associations, in heraldry black, called *sable*, stands for the virtues of constancy, prudence, and wisdom. This may have been the rationale for calling England's Edward *the Black Prince*, but more of him later. And while black may be benign in heraldic devices, in flags and ensigns it is associated with deadliness and death.

Soon after light-skinned Europeans first laid eyes on Africans and other dark-skinned peoples, they called them "black." One of the first appearances of this terminology in print was in a travel book of 1625, describing "The mouth of the river, where dwell the Blackes, called Mandingos." In subsequent eras the words "colored" and "Negro" came to be considered less offensive, but about the middle of the twentieth century there was a turnaround, and these terms were considered veiled insults by those who insisted that *black is beautiful*. Currently this view is changing again, and "black" is being displaced, at least in America, by "Afro-American," "African American," and "people of color." (Also see BLACKAMOOR below.)

✿ *As Black as* . . . ✿

Just then flew down a monstrous crow,
As black as a tar-barrel;

—LEWIS CARROLL,
Through the Looking-Glass (1872)

Proverbial similes involving the color black abound. As *black as a crow* or *raven* dates from Roman times. According to Roman legend, ravens originally were pure white until one day a raven complained to Apollo of the faithlessness of a nymph he loved. Apollo shot the nymph but punished the raven for squealing by changing his color to black. Joseph Addison's translation of Ovid has it:

He blacked the raven o'er,
And bid him prate in his white plumes no more.

Chaucer expanded on the simile to include coal ("As blak as any cole or crowe," *The Knight's Tale*), presumably more in the interests of meter than explication, whereas Shakespeare left it at crow ("Black as e'er was crow," *The Winter's Tale*, 4:4).

The *four-and-twenty blackbirds* baked in the famous nursery-rhyme pie were definitely not crows (as in "eating crow"), for "when the pie was opened the birds began to sing," a talent conspicuously absent in crows. Yet in folklore *blackbirds*, like crows and ravens, are symbols of bad luck and evil. In nineteenth-century slang blackbirds were Negro or Polynesian captives on slave ships, and *blackbirding* meant kidnapping blacks for slavery.

The principal vegetable similes for blackness are the *sloe*, the small, sour, bluish-black fruit of the blackthorn, and the *blackberry*. They appear together in the thirteenth-century translation of the *Roman de la Rose*, thought to have been made by Chaucer: "Blak as bery, or any slo." Chaucer used "black as sloe" again in *The Miller's Tale*, but it has become less common in modern parlance. The blackberry, on the other hand, has appeared in another simile popular since Shakespeare wrote, "Give you a reason on compulsion! if reasons were as *plentiful as blackberries* [emphasis added] I would give no man a reason upon compulsion" (*King Henry IV*, Part 1, 2:4). In England, at least, a blackberry harvest is reputedly huge. This fruit also gave rise to the term *blackberry summer*, the British equivalent of the North American Indian summer—that is, fine weather in late September and early October, when the blackberries are ripe. And the tree that bears sloes gave rise to *blackthorn winter*, an unseasonable cold spell in late April and early May, when the blackthorn is blooming.

Of the inorganic substances appearing in simile, *pitch* is among the oldest. "Blacker than pitch" appears in Homer's *Iliad* (c. 850 B.C.), and *black as pitch* occurs again and again in writings to the present day. A Chinese proverb in William Scarborough's 1875 compendium says "Black as pitch and ink," and indeed the latter comparison appears in English from the early sixteenth century until the twentieth, when ink was no longer invariably black. Black as *jet, soot*, and *ebony* all are equally old. Older still is the aforementioned *black as coal*, which the *OED* cites as early as c. 1000. A Saxon manuscript predating the year 1000 has "Swa sweart swa col," and it may have been proverbial even then. Chaucer used this one again and again, and it remains current.

Long before people began to worry about pollution,

coal also acquired the nickname *black diamonds*, alluding to its undisputed value as a fuel, and perhaps also referring to the two substances' common origin as a form of carbon. Ralph Waldo Emerson so called it in his essay on *Wealth* (1860):

> *We may well call it black diamonds. Every basket is power and civilization. For coal is a portable climate. It carries the heat of the tropics to Labrador and the polar circle; and it is the means of transporting itself whithersoever it is wanted.*

Gourmets sometimes use "black diamonds" to mean truffles, considered at least as precious as these minerals and similarly found underground.

Yet another natural substance is *black frost*, as frost not accompanied by rime (white ice particles) has been called since the fourteenth century. It is similar but not quite identical to *black ice*, a term that came into use only in the nineteenth century and refers specifically to a coating of hard, very thin, transparent ice over a road surface. Because it cannot readily be seen, black ice is extremely dangerous to motorists and pedestrians, who, not realizing that a road is icy, do not proceed with the care they might use if they were aware of it. Oceanographers also use "black ice" to describe sea ice that is clear enough to show the water underneath it.

> *Out of the night that covers me,*
> *Black as the Pit from pole to pole . . .*
>
> —WILLIAM ERNEST HENLEY,
> *Invictus* (1875)

In addition to similes alluding to animals, plants, and minerals, looser associations abound. *Black as night* seems a fairly obvious comparison. *Black as hell, Hades,*

and *the devil* were common to the point of being clichés
until the relatively recent past and hence were sometimes
picturesquely embellished. In this vein were "blak as
feend in helle" (*Roman de la Rose*, c. 1340), "black as the
devil's hind foot" (T. C. Haliburton in Sam Slick's *Wise
Saws* of 1843), and countless others. As seen above, William Ernest Henley avoided "hell" altogether, substitut-
ing "the Pit."

The rationale for *black as thunder* is puzzling unless
it is interpreted as alluding to thunderclouds. Nevertheless, William Makepeace Thackeray used it a number of
times ("Black as thunder looked King Padella" in *The
Rose and the Ring* of 1855 is but one instance), as did
numerous later writers. *Black as the ace of spades* and
black as a minister's coat, both nineteenth-century Amer-
icanisms, are obviously descriptive, but the contemporary
American usage of *black as your/my hat* is less clear, since
hats neither were nor are always black.

🙄 *The Black Death* 🙄

White is love, and black is death.

—J. O. HALLIWELL,
Nursery Rhymes of England (1842)

The Great Pestilence of 1348 and 1349, which ravaged
Europe and killed approximately 12 percent of England's
population, was what is now called bubonic plague. An
acute and severe infection, bubonic plague is caused by
the bacillus *Yersinia pestis*, which is transmitted from
rodents to humans by the bite of an infected flea. Un-
treated, it causes death in about 60 percent of patients
today and probably had a much higher mortality rate in
the fourteenth century, when general health was much

poorer. Death generally occurs within three to five days of infection.

The name *Black Death* does not appear in the literature of the time but showed up in print only many years later, in 1823, in an account by a Mrs. Markham. She is thought to have adopted the term from Danish and Swedish chroniclers who had used it in the sixteenth century. Exactly what it refers to is not known, but it alludes either to the devastating nature of the epidemic or to the darkening of a patient's skin when the underlying buboes (enlarged infected lymph nodes characteristic of the disease) hemorrhaged.

"Black" turns up in a number of other unpleasant medical conditions, ranging from the common and relatively harmless *blackhead* and *black eye* to the potentially fatal illnesses known as *blackwater fever* and *black lung*. Although it can be the bane of adolescents worried about their acne, a blackhead is simply an open comedo, a small, black-tipped fatty mass in a skin follicle. It is unsightly but basically innocuous. The name "blackhead," which describes it perfectly, has been used since the early nineteenth century. Blackwater fever, on the other hand, is a dangerous form of malaria in which the patient's urine turns dark (brown or blue-black) in color, signifying severe kidney damage. This term, too, dates from the nineteenth century, when malaria afflicted thousands of Europeans who moved from temperate zones to the tropics, where this parasitic disease is endemic.

Black lung disease is a legacy of the industrial revolution, when enormously increased demand for fossil fuels led to the vast expansion of the coal mining industry. Indeed, the current official medical term for this disease is "coal workers' pneumoconiosis." It is characterized by the deposition of coal dust in the lungs as a result of long-term exposure to either bituminous or anthracite coal dust. The condition is revealed only by X rays and does not invariably give rise to respiratory symptoms in its early stages. By the time it does hamper breathing significantly, it is generally too late to reverse its course.

Black bile, which sounds like a fatal disease, is actually one of the four elemental bodily humors distinguished by medieval physiologists and simply refers to gloominess or melancholy. The Latin writer Cicero may have been the first to refer to it. John de Trevisa, translator of a Latin treatise entitled *The Property of Things* (1398), wrote,

> *Malencoly is bred of trowbled draft of blode and hath his name of melon that is black and calor that is humour, so is said as it were a blak humour.*

And three centuries later a medical dictionary by John Quincy had it, "Melancholy, supposed to proceed from a Redundance of black Bile" (*Lexicon Phisico-Medicum*, 1722).

A *black heart* is wholly figurative, on the other hand, signifying a person's evil nature. James Kelly included it in his Scottish proverb collection of 1721, "It is ill to put a blithe face on a black heart."

> *Mistress Ford, good heart, is*
> *beaten black and blue.*
>
> —WILLIAM SHAKESPEARE,
> *The Merry Wives of Windsor*, 4:5

Black and blue, for badly bruised, has been in use since about 1300. Bruises do take on various colors, though pure black is rarely one of them. Presumably the alliteration helped perpetuate the term, which is used just as frequently today. It also may be used somewhat figuratively, as it was by Joseph G. Baldwin in 1853, "He cursed them black and blue" (*The Flush Times of Alabama and Mississippi*), here meaning simply with extreme vigor.

> *Cussed himself black in the face.*
>
> —MARK TWAIN, *A Tramp Abroad* (1879)

Blackwater or black lung may be reason to call on the medical establishment, but being *black in the face* merely refers to extreme physical effort or violent passion. This particular expression has been around since the early nineteenth century. Charles Dickens's Mr. Winkle "pulled till he was black in the face" (*Pickwick Papers*, 1836), and on the other side of the Atlantic, Charles F. Browne wrote, "He kept on larfin till he was black in the face" (*Artemus Ward His Travels*, 1862).

Of course, physical effort can be carried too far, causing one *to black out*. To lose consciousness is one of the most recent meanings of this term, which actually dates from the fifteenth century, when it meant to stain or to defame (probably from figuratively "blackening" a person's name or reputation). Later it acquired several other meanings—to obliterate with black (the *OED* first cites this meaning in print in 1850); to extinguish lights in a theater (1920s); and finally to lose consciousness. In the theater it referred to turning out the lights during a scene change, but during World War II *blackout* took on a more sinister meaning: the darkening of a city to protect it against enemy bombs. Applying the term to loss of consciousness is thought to have originated with pilots who experienced a temporary faint before pulling out of a power dive. Today *blackout* also refers to memory loss, from any number of causes, as well as to a breakdown in communications, such as a *news blackout*, or a loss of electricity, termed a *power blackout*.

*And I'm here in the Clink for a thundering drink
and blacking the Corporal's eye.*

—RUDYARD KIPLING, *Cells* (1892)

A *black eye* is a not very accurate description of the dis-
colored flesh around the eye that results from a blow or
contusion. The term has been around since at least 1604,
when Thomas Dekker had it in his play *The Honest
Whore*. It also has been used figuratively, since the early
fifteenth century, to mean shame or dishonor, principally
in such phrases as *black is his eye*, meaning he is at fault
or to blame. Somewhat later, *giving someone a black eye*
began to be used in the sense of giving a severe blow or
rebuff, and by extension a black eye came to mean defeat
or discouragement. This usage became common on both
sides of the Atlantic. "Massachusetts beaten; and a black
eye for Connecticut," editorialized *The Massachusetts Spy*
in 1795. In the course of time the term became figurative
to the point of absurdity, as when Senator McHamilton
of Texas said in 1876, "Somebody was threatening to give
a black eye to these 3.65 bonds."

More accurately descriptive uses of "black eye" appear in at least two American plant names. The *black-
eyed Susan* is a common name for the species *Rudbeckia
hirta*, a daisylike flower with a very dark center disk that
is the state flower of Maryland. And *black-eyed pea* is a
common name for the cowpea, a staple of southern American cooking.

Black figures descriptively in plant and animal pa-
thology as well. *Black spot*, dreaded by gardeners, is a
nasty fungus that affects fruit trees and ornamental
plants, especially roses. It is characterized by dark spots
that show first on the leaves, which eventually will drop,
and on the fruit, which then rots. According to Eric Partridge's compendium of underworld slang, "black spot"

also is (or was) criminal lingo for an alias, but this is hardly in general use today, if ever it was.

Domestic animals, on the other hand, suffer from *blackleg*, an infectious and often fatal disease; it is caused by a soil bacterium, *Clostridium chauvoei*, and characterized by painful swellings in the upper part of the leg. A scourge of cattle and sheep, it can be treated successfully with antibiotics. This name, too, became a slang expression, primarily in Great Britain, where in the eighteenth century a blackleg was a swindler on the racecourse or in gambling, and in the nineteenth century a strikebreaker or scab (an employee who continues to work for an employer against whom others are striking). The origin of these usages has been lost.

🔊 *Baa, Baa, Black Sheep, Have You Any Wool?* 🔊

The familiar nursery rhyme alludes quite straightforwardly to a sheep whose wool is black, and indeed "black" attached to various animal names most often is merely describing their color, dark if not actually pure black. Certainly this is true of the black fly, black squirrel, black ant, black duck, and several dozen others. In some cases, however, figurative meanings have attached themselves as well.

One of the oldest and best known is that same *black sheep*, which John Lyly described in his *Endimion* (1591) as a "perilous beast," a description that had also appeared in the *Percy Ballads* of c. 1550 ("a black sheep is a perilous [biting] beast"). One could safely say that black sheep present no greater danger than their lighter-colored cohorts, but it is true that black sheep were considered less valuable because their wool could not be dyed as readily as white wool, a fact already pointed out by the Roman writer Pliny in his *Natural History* (A.D. 77). Moreover, most domestic sheep range in color from white to light brown, so the rare black sheep in a flock came to be regarded as more or less a freak of nature. Perhaps for this reason, in witchcraft black lambs sometimes were sacrificed to Hecate at a crossroads, where this goddess's image would be placed as a charm against evil spirits. From the early seventeenth century on, *to know someone from a black sheep* meant to identify a deceiver or an untrustworthy person. This usage is now obsolete, but since the eighteenth century we have described individuals who are oddly different from their fellows, the least successful or least admirable members of a group, as black sheep. Sir Walter Scott wrote, "The curates know best the black sheep of their flock" (*Old Mortality*, 1816), and the family black sheep likewise became a common way of singling out the odd member. The term did not necessarily signify evil or wrongdoing; a black sheep was simply different from the rest.

Another straightforward descriptive name is *black snake*, the common name for several species of very dark-colored reptiles. In mid-nineteenth-century America, however, this name came to be also used for a long, cruel whip made of braided cowhide or some similar flexible material. "In the midst of it all, he would start up with a sudden yell of anguish, whirl his black snake, and let fly at the mules," wrote J. Ross Browne (*Adventures in the Apache Country*, 1869).

Some superstitious individuals still regard the sight of a *black cat* as unlucky. During the Middle Ages many believed that Satan often took the form of a black cat, leading to the idea that a black cat was the devil's "familiar"—his slave or companion. In the witchcraft trials of sixteenth-century England and seventeenth-century Massachusetts, the presence of a black cat in company with the accused was sometimes cited as evidence of her guilt.

The term *black dog*, on the other hand, has been used since the late eighteenth century to signify sadness or a bad mood. Sir Walter Scott had it in *Antiquary* (1816): "Sir Arthur has got the black dog on his back again." (In modern parlance we have dropped the dog entirely and substituted another color; see THE BLUES.) And as far as expressing negative feelings are concerned, we still use *black look* to signify a frown or other kind of angry look. Jane Austen used this in *Mansfield Park* (1814), "My brother-in-law looked rather black upon me," and today a black look still bodes ill for those on the receiving end of it.

🐾 *Blackamoor* 🐾

I care not an she were a black-a-moor.

> —WILLIAM SHAKESPEARE,
> *Troilus and Cressida*, 1:1

Archaic as *blackamoor* may sound today, both "Moor" and "Ethiopian" long were the standard appellations for dark-skinned Africans and other foreigners. Aesop wrote a fable (c. 570 B.C.) about a man who bought a black slave and, thinking his color was caused by dirt, tried to scrub it off. The fable gave rise to a proverb quoted by Erasmus, and the idea was repeated many times over the years. In the early seventeenth century, the English playwrights Thomas Dekker and William Wycherley each referred to it in several plays, using the word "blackamoor," which is thought to come simply from combining "black" and Moor. As late as 1853 J. R. Planche, discussing the famous antislavery novel *Uncle Tom's Cabin*, wrote, "If any one could wash a blackamoor white, it would be Mrs. Beecher Stowe." Today, of course, the term is considered not only archaic but also offensive. Meanwhile, thousands of miles across the Pacific, Australian settlers referred to the indigenous population there, the aborigines, as *blackfellows*, a term today considered as offensive as "blackamoor."

Despite the fact that native African skin is no more black than northern European skin is pure white, these color words have been used to differentiate the two races for hundreds of years. In countries with both a sizable black and white population, such as the United States, various words for describing those of African descent— black, Negro, colored, African-American—have at different times and by different groups been considered polite or derogatory. For example, in the mid-nineteenth century the epithet *black Republican* was used by their opponents (southern Democrats) for members of the Republican Party who were thought to favor Negroes and the abolition of slavery. Depending on one's politics, it was either an insult or a compliment.

An extremely popular form of nineteenth-century American entertainment, the minstrel show, involved *blackface*—white performers blackened their faces with burned cork and performed what they perceived to be Negro songs, dances, and skits. (Incidentally, in Chinese drama, which involves heavy use of makeup for symbolic purposes, an actor in blackface represents a rough, honest individual.)

Another nineteenth-century Americanism is *black belt*, used in two senses in the latter part of the century. One meaning alluded to black "bottomland," fertile dark soil in various parts of the South that is ideal for growing cotton. The other referred to areas with a large Negro population. It was defined by Alabama Senator John T. Morgan, expressing his prejudice in the U.S. Senate in 1878: "There is one region of country to which no man emigrates, and that is what is called 'the black belt,' where the negro population is very dense." Today, however, the term brings to mind a quite different meaning: the highest rank of expertise in judo and karate, which entitles those who achieve it to wear a black belt. The term has been so used since about 1910.

In the early twentieth century the above-described fertile bottomland sometimes was referred to as *black bottom*. In 1926, however, a song called "Black Bottom" was introduced in a popular Broadway show, *George White's Scandals*, along with a dance routine devised by White. "Black bottom" is thought to have referred to the muddy bottomland, and the dance movements to dragging one's feet through the mud. The song, particularly as performed by Alberta Hunter, helped make the dance wildly popular in ballrooms throughout America.

As was pointed out earlier, "black" for "Negro" came to be considered insulting and was replaced, at least for a time, by "Negro" and "colored." About the middle of the twentieth century, however, this attitude changed yet again. *Black is beautiful* became the slogan of the *black power* movement, that is, the concerted effort of American blacks to develop their own political and social institutions and foster pride in their history and culture. It is no longer clear just who invented the names for these outgrowths of the 1960s civil rights movement, but they were still new when Adam Clayton Powell wrote an essay in 1967 entitled "Black Power: A Form of Godly Power" (in *Keep the Faith, Baby!*). At about this same time the name *Black Panthers* began to be used for a militant organization promoting black power. The *San Francisco Examiner* mentioned that "SNCC [Student Nonviolent Coordinating Committee] has chosen a black panther to adorn its party emblem" (December 1965). By 1966 the name was familiar enough that the British journal *The Economist* referred to the organization as the Black Panthers. A somewhat earlier development was the organization of the *Black Muslims*, established in 1931 by "Wallace Farad" and developed further by Elijah Muhammad. This radical movement rejected Christianity as a white religion and replaced it with a form of Islam. Preaching the separation of blacks and whites, it reached a peak of influence in the United States during the 1960s under the leadership of Malcolm X, who was assassinated in 1965.

Although the ultimate goals of economic, political, and social equality have not, at this writing, been fully met, by the 1990s the names of these radical movements were heard less often. Furthermore, in the United States the appellation "black" was increasingly being replaced by "Afro-American," "African-American," and people "of color."

🐦 *Black Magic* 🐦

That old black magic has me in its spell,
That old black magic that you weave so well.

—JOHNNY MERCER (1942)

The fanciful description of love in Harold Arlen and Johnny Mercer's popular song (from the musical *Star-Spangled Rhythm*) is far from the original meaning of *black magic*—sorcery or witchcraft involving the invocation of devils and other evil spirits. The *OED* cites anthropologist E. B. Tylor's mention of it in his *Primitive Culture* (1871), "What with slavery and what with black magic, life is precarious among the Wakhutu." This term replaced the earlier *black art*, which is thought to have entered the language as a translation of the Low German *swarte Kunst*. In English it appeared in the sixteenth century. Christopher Marlowe had it in his play *Doctor Faustus* (c. 1590): "I have heard strange report of thy knowledge of the black art" (Scene 10).

A close relative of these terms is the *Black Mass*, a travesty of the Christian rite in which Satan rather than God is invoked, and various obscene rites are performed in place of the solemn sacred ceremony. (However, this same term is also sometimes used to mean a genuine Requiem Mass, a Mass said for the dead.)

And did you not hear of a jolly young waterman,
Who at Blackfriars Bridge used for to ply;

—CHARLES DIBDIN (1745–1814), *The Waterman*

Another straightforward descriptive use of black is in *Black Friars*, the name used since the fifteenth century or so for the Dominican order, who wear a distinctive black mantle. This name then was transferred to the district of London in which their convent used to be located, including its bridge across the Thames, referred to in Dibdin's poem.

Religious associations involving black are not confined to Christianity. The *Black Stone* is kissed by every pilgrim who comes to the Kaaba at Mecca. Muslim legend holds that it was white when it fell from heaven but was turned black by the sins of mankind. The stone predates Muslim times; the ancient Persians worshiped it as the emblem of Saturn.

❧ *The Black Prince* ❧

Brave Gaunt, thy father and myself
Rescued the Black Prince, that young Mars of men,
From forth the ranks of many thousand French.

—WILLIAM SHAKESPEARE, *Richard II*, 2:3

Edward, Prince of Wales, the eldest son of Edward III, was known as the Black Prince, but no one knows exactly why. A valiant military leader, he may have been so called because he wore black armor. Or perhaps the heraldic virtues symbolized by the color black (prudence, wisdom, constancy) were assigned to this prince. In any event, he was so described by sixteenth-century chroniclers, notably Grafton and Holinshed, and Shakespeare perpetuated the name in at least two of his plays.

His father, King Edward III, is remembered for *Black Monday*, the day of his defeat by the French in the siege of Paris. Supposedly that occurred on Easter Monday, April 14, 1360, a day so bitterly cold and windy that many men and horses died. However, the chroniclers who gave it this name were careless with their calendars, for in fact April 14 of that year fell on a Tuesday. Nevertheless, Black Monday continued to signify the Monday after Easter, either in allusion to this event or, more likely, from the superstition that the joyousness of Easter was necessarily followed by calamity. British schoolchildren also use the term for the first Monday following a vacation.

In more recent times, journalists used the name Black Monday for October 19, 1987, a day when the New York stock market fell sharply and the Dow Jones Industrial Average declined by more than 500 points. The allusion here, however, was to the stock-market collapse of October 29, 1929, which was dubbed *Black Friday* and is often considered to mark the start of the Great Depression.

Either Black Monday or Black Friday might readily be called a *black-letter day*, a term used for any inauspicious day of the calendar. This term comes from the fact that saints' days and other holidays were traditionally marked in red on the church calendar, where black then represented a marked contrast to joyful or celebratory occasions. Or, as Tobias Smollett put it in his poem *Reprisal* (1757),

> *O! the month of November,*
> *She'll have to remember,*
> *As a black-letter day all the days of her life.*

✒ *The Black Hole* ✒

Black also is associated with several infamous historic events. Outstanding among them is the so-called *Black Hole of Calcutta*. On the night of June 20, 1756, the Nawab of Bengal confined 146 European prisoners in a small prison in the East India Company's Fort William, which his forces had captured. By morning only twenty-three prisoners were still alive, the others having suffocated in the fourteen-by-eighteen-foot space. The precise details of this event have been questioned by modern historians, some of whom conclude that it never took place at all but was a piece of British propaganda. Nevertheless, the name survives along with the apocryphal story, and further, *black hole* continues to mean a dungeon, solitary cell, or other kind of lockup. In the 1960s astronomers transferred this term to describe a region or massive theoretical object where gravity is so strong that no matter or radiation can escape from it, presumably alluding to a prison cell from which escape is impossible.

Even less merciful than a dungeon cell is the *black*

flag, which has signified death or a deadly purpose since
the Middle Ages. It was used by besieging forces to indicate they would take no prisoners but kill all their
enemies (perhaps in contrast to the white flag used to
signify surrender). Thomas Nashe wrote in 1593, "The
black flag was set up, which signified there was no mercy
to be looked for." A version of it was adopted by pirates,
who embellished the plain black cloth with a white skull
and crossbones. It was called the "Jolly Roger," whence
the name *black Roger* for a pirate.

Although pirates plied most of the earth's oceans and
seas, they were more of a threat on the Mediterranean,
Atlantic, and Pacific than on the *Black Sea*, which lies
between Europe and Asia. There are numerous theories
concerning the origin of its name, which was Pontus Eux-
inus (Euxine Sea) in Roman times. One is that the Turks
so named it because of its danger to ships. Another holds
that it was named for its position north of Turkey, for in
the Turkish language the color black is associated with
the direction north. And still another linguist suggests
that the name is purely descriptive—that is, the waters
are very dark—and was already so used by the ancient
Greeks, who called it Pontes Melas.

> *Before the organization of the Black-Shirt move-
> ment free speech did not exist in this country.*
>
> —SIR OSWALD MOSLEY

Probably feared even more than pirates were the modern-
day *Black Shirts*, as various Fascist organizations have
been called (for the black shirt of their uniforms). The
first among them were Benito Mussolini's followers in
Italy in the 1920s, and soon afterward the name was used
in Germany for Adolf Hitler's elite Nazi corps, the *Schutz-
staffel* ("defense squadron"), or S.S. for short. These
groups had sympathizers in Great Britain and America,

some of whom copied their uniforms. Among them was the above-quoted Sir Oswald Mosley, who had founded a Fascist organization in Britain in 1932, was an outspoken supporter of the Nazis, and consequently spent much of World War II in internment.

A decade or so before Mosley founded his group came the *Black and Tans*, a special British force recruited in 1921 to help the Royal Irish Constabulary put down the Sinn Fein rebellion in Ireland. They were so called for their uniform, which combined the army khaki (tan) with the constabulary's black caps and belts. They became infamous for their use of needless force. Although their efforts actually were defeated when negotiations resulted in the establishment of the Irish Free State (now the Republic of Ireland), their association with violence was not forgotten, and their name continued to be invoked in numerous subsequent Anglo-Irish conflicts. (In the nineteenth century, *black and tan*, in the singular and lowercase, also referred to a kind of dog, a terrier with a black back and tan face, flank, and legs, as well as being slang for a drink that combined porter or stout with ale.)

Similarly associated with nefarious deeds was the *Black Hand*, a name used for several much-feared groups. The best known of them was a secret society of Italian immigrants who brought their criminal activities from Sicily to the United States around the turn of the twentieth century. It was known particularly for sending *blackmail* letters that threatened the victim with death and were marked with a picture of a black hand. Among the crimes for which the Black Hand was held responsible was the murder of the New Orleans chief of police in 1890 and the shooting of a New York City policeman in Palermo, Sicily, in 1909.

The word *blackmail*, however, comes from sixteenth-century Scotland, where it denoted the tribute exacted from farmers and landowners on the English border by freebooting chiefs in return for protection from plunder.

Mail is a Scottish word for a payment, and *black* referred to the fact that it usually took the form of grain, cattle, or other goods rather than "white" silver money. (*Black money* once meant copper or debased silver coins, but this usage is obsolete.)

> *What have I ever done to you young blackguards,*
> *that you should treat me thus?*
>
> —FREDERICK W. FARRAR, *Eric* (1858)

In a later era the chieftains' victims might have called these extortionists *blackguards*, but in their day this term, which came to mean a rogue or a scoundrel, had a different meaning. In the sixteenth century a blackguard was a menial or camp follower who looked after the dirtiest household chores—dealing with filthy black pots, coal fires, and the like. John Webster used this description in his play *The White Devil* (c. 1608):

> *A lousy slave, that within this twenty years rode*
> *with the black guard in the Duke's carriage,*
> *'mongst spits and dripping pans!*

In the seventeenth century the word, in the singular, began to be applied to criminals as a body, and from the early eighteenth century on it began to be used in its present meaning. The historian Thomas Macaulay defined it, rather stuffily, in 1830: "A man whose manners and sentiments are decidedly below those of his class deserves to be called a blackguard." Although the word was widely used in America, where at one time it was converted to a verb that meant "to use vile language," it has a distinctly old-fashioned or archaic ring and is not much heard today.

~ *You're in My Black Book!* ~

Blackguards deserve to be in someone's *black book*, a much older locution that remains current. Today it most often simply means that someone is out of favor. Beginning as early as the fourteenth century, there have been numerous black books with more specific meanings. The first of these to list persons to be censured or punished was a series of reports presented to Parliament in 1536 that had been compiled by the agents of King Henry VIII. It consisted of a list of English monasteries that were described as "sinful." Henry's motives, of course, were worldly rather than spiritual; he wanted Parliament to dissolve all the monasteries in order to acquire their large holdings of land for the crown.

By the late sixteenth century the term was being used more generally for any listing of faults or offenders. Thus the *Oxford Dictionary of Proverbs* cites Robert Greene, writing in 1592, "Ned Browne's villanies . . . are too many to be described in my Blacke Booke." But the older meaning was retained in black books compiled by the British police, army, universities, and other institutions that kept lists of offenders. An eighteenth-century history of Oxford University describes a proctor's black book that, if a person's name was listed in it, prevented him from proceeding to a university degree.

In the twentieth century the term acquired another, far less ominous meaning. In one of the popular musical films in which Fred Astaire starred with Ginger Rogers, Astaire tried to make his leading lady jealous by extolling the charms of the pretty girls listed in his *little black notebook*. Many a bachelor imitated this practice, or at least this terminology, referring to his current telephone directory of girlfriends as "his little black book." The older meaning has persisted as well, however, and *being in someone's black book* still means being out of favor.

Once Blackballed, Romania Joins the Aid Club

—HEADLINE, *The New York Times*,
January 31, 1991

Similar meanings are attached to being *blackballed* or on a *blacklist*. The practice of blacklisting persons who have incurred suspicion or censure or are to be punished dates from approximately 1600. The term acquired a more specific meaning in the latter half of the nineteenth century, when it referred to a list of workmen considered undesirable by an employer on account of their union membership or activities. Sometimes such workers countered by creating a blacklist of their own, of employers whom union members refused to work for. The blacklist acquired particularly sinister connotations during the McCarthy hearings of the early 1950s, when numerous actors, entertainers, and writers accused (often quite falsely) of being Communists were blacklisted by employers and were unable to find work.

The *Times* headline above announces Romania's entrance into an economic aid program from which it had been excluded on account of its government's repressive measures against protesters some months earlier. Literally using a black ball to exclude someone dates from the eighteenth century, when votes against a candidate were cast by putting black balls in the ballot box (favorable votes were cast with a red or white ball). By about 1840 or so the term had been extended to mean any sort of exclusion or ostracism.

A similar sign of disfavor is a *black mark* against someone. While this term, too, originally meant literally placing a cross or other mark against the name of someone who had incurred censure or a penalty, it was being used figuratively by the mid-nineteenth century, as it still is. Benjamin Disraeli included it in his novel *Sybil*

(1845): "I see you, Mrs. Page. Won't there be a black mark against you?"

Writing in black is not always a bad thing. On the contrary, being *in the black* is considered highly desirable, especially when compared with its opposite, *in the red*. Since the 1920s or so, in the black has signified showing a profit or being out of debt, as opposed to showing a loss. Both terms come from the conventional accounting practice of inscribing credits in black ink and debits in red. Despite the fact that computerized accounting does not follow this convention, the terms survive.

> *Those that eat black pudding will dream of the devil.*
>
> —JONATHAN SWIFT, *Polite Conversation* (1738)

Black pudding is a typical British sausage made of meat, blood, and suet. It is more often called "blood sausage" in America, although the British name is used in the South. It is very dark in color but not precisely black.

The same is true of several other edible substances. *Black coffee*, preferred by many caffeine aficionados, is simply strong coffee served without adding milk or cream; the name has been used since the late eighteenth century. *Blackstrap* is a name used in Great Britain for two quite different drinks—port wine of inferior quality, and a mixture of rum and treacle (Americans call the latter molasses). In America in the early nineteenth century this name was used for any cheap liquor and later also for a mixture of molasses with rum or whiskey, which was sometimes drunk as a kind of medicinal tonic. Much more appealing, in both name and flavor, is *black velvet*, a mixture of half champagne and half stout. The stout, a strong, rather sweet brew, is very dark in color, and the champagne adds a velvety smoothness to the drink.

In the late sixteenth century a *blackjack* was a large leather jug or drinking cup that was coated with tar or some other very dark-colored material to make it watertight for its contents, traditionally beer or ale. Somewhat later this name was used for the caramel used to darken the color of spirits, vinegar, and other liquids. It also was a variant for the black pirate flag (see BLACK FLAG). It was only in the late nineteenth century that it acquired the two meanings most current today: (1) a weapon consisting of a short, leather-covered truncheon, with a heavy head and flexible handle, and (2) a gambling game originally called *vingt-et-un* (French for "twenty-one").

Either kind of modern blackjack, the weapon or the gambling game, might cause the arrival of a *black Maria*, as a police patrol wagon for rounding up the drunk and disorderly has been called in America since the mid-nineteenth century. No one knows for sure why a paddy wagon should be so called, but there is a legend that it was named for Maria Lee, a large and very strong woman who kept a boardinghouse for sailors on the Boston waterfront. When her boarders got out of hand and she was unable to control them, she sent for constables to take them to jail, and hence the horse-drawn wagon they used, usually black in color, came to be named for her. Although the story is apocryphal and the vehicles used for this purpose have long since changed, the name has survived.

> *Under the spreading chestnut tree*
> *The village smithy stands;*
> *The smith, a mighty man is he,*
> *With large and sinewy hands.*
>
> —HENRY WADSWORTH LONGFELLOW,
> *The Village Blacksmith* (1841)

Longfellow's famous poem romanticizes the *blacksmith*, a worker so called since the fifteenth century because he works in *black metal*, as iron was once called (*smith* simply meant metalworker). Longfellow was not the first to take such a view. An air by George Frideric Handel was, some time after the composer's death in 1759, named *The Harmonious Blacksmith* because it was allegedly inspired by a particular blacksmith named William Powell working at his forge.

Blacksmiths are no longer numerous, but their name has survived. And iron is no longer called "black metal," although its color has not changed. The *blackboard*, however, is still so called, even though it today rarely consists of the very dark slate of which it was always made in the early nineteenth century, when it acquired this name. Today it is also called, with somewhat more accuracy, a "chalkboard," and consists of any smooth and hard material on which a lecturer or teacher can write with chalk. It also survives in the term *blackboard jungle*, which originally was the title of a 1954 novel by Evan Hunter about a school characterized by lack of discipline and juvenile delinquency. The term was quickly adopted to describe any such school or school system.

In modern inner-city schools drugs are not only something carried in a doctor's *black bag* but occasionally are talked of as a *black bomber* or a *black beauty*. The black bomber became a slang name for amphetamines, mainly in Britain during the 1960s; in America black beauty was slang for a particular brand of amphetamine that came in a black capsule. Even the black bag, traditionally a physician's leather bag that was carried along on house calls (which themselves verge on obsolescence), has acquired criminal associations. It sometimes alludes to a fund that has been diverted from a regular budget for dubious, if not illegal, purposes. And further, in America in the 1970s it was used to describe illegal entry or other activity by government agents in search of evidence (called *a black-bag job*).

Unfortunately, illegal substances are all too readily available to youngsters, on a widely accessible *black market*. This term, meaning illegal dealing in rationed goods or unauthorized imports, originated during World War I. It is thought to have been a translation of the German *Schwarzmarkt*, which meant illicit sales of rationed goods, and was revived during World War II with the same meaning. After the war, the meaning was expanded to include items smuggled into the country to evade customs duties or in contravention of the law.

Any color you like so long as it's black.

—HENRY FORD

The remark above, attributed to Henry Ford in offering his Model T car to American buyers, caught on as a catchphrase meaning "That's all there is; take it or leave it." While Ford may never have actually uttered these words, there is no doubt that, being an extremely shrewd businessman, he deliberately chose black as the color for all his cars. To take full advantage of the economies of mass production, only one color was feasible. Further, black paint was cheap and durable. And finally, black not only "goes with" anything but was considered elegant as well. So all the model T's that rolled off that early assembly line were black.

The idea of black as elegant survives in the *black tie* and the *little black dress*. The practice of wearing a black bow tie with a dinner jacket for evening dress dates from the mid-nineteenth century. Thus C. M. Yonge wrote, "Tom . . . had sent on his black tie and agate studs" (*Daisy Chain*, 1856). And today we still talk of a black-tie affair when we mean one where formal evening dress is required.

Far from the plain black dress of a widow's weeds, the little black dress is a fashion idea of the twentieth century. From the late 1930s on, a simple, fairly plain black dress, stylishly cut but of street length (not floor length), was touted as an essential part of a woman's wardrobe. Representing the height of understated good taste, such attire would, said the fashion designers, make a woman look well dressed in any setting. Although the idea might seem old-fashioned to some, a *New York Times* article of 1991, discussing the remarkable expansion of denim production, bore the headline "The Little Black Denim Dress."

The pot calls the kettle burnt-arse.

—JOHN CLARKE, *Paroemiologia* (1639)

Here is one of the earliest versions of an age-old saying concerning faultfinders who are as much in the wrong as those they criticize. Today we usually put it as "the pot calling the kettle black." The same pot was at one time called "black-brows" by the kettle, a 1620 version of the same adage.

🐌 *Black and White* 🐌

A similar fallacy often pointed out in proverbs is that of confusing black and white, in which black usually represents evil and white good. Thus a book review in the London *Observer* of 1974 said, "Like the slag-heap calling the polar bear black." Some 450 years earlier it was "Makyng as he lyst blacke of whyte." But the same idea had been expressed by the Latin poet Ovid in his *Metamorphoses* (A.D. 7), "Well skilled in cunning wiles, he could make white of black and black of white."

Not everyone believes that the good-evil dichotomy should rule one's view of the world. Thus George Canning warned, in his *New Morality*,

> *And finds, with keen discriminating sight,*
> *Black's not so black;—nor white so very white.*

Black and white have long been linguistically paired in another way. "What's black and white and re[a]d all over?" says the old schoolyard riddle, which is slightly more puzzling when spoken aloud. The traditional answer, "A newspaper," echoes one of the oldest meanings for *in black and white*—that is, recorded in writing or print. Chaucer used it in this way in the fourteenth century. John Bunyan had it in his *Pilgrim's Progress* (1678):

> *Thus I set pen to paper with delight,*
> *And quickly had my thoughts in black and white.*

And, of course, it remains current. Moreover, from the late nineteenth century on, with the development of color photography, *black and white* was used to distinguish certain artwork, film, and television from color media.

There are other figurative uses of black and white, such as chocolate and vanilla (for example, a vanilla ice-cream soda with chocolate ice cream), or coffee (black) to which milk or cream (white) has been added.

> *I prefer my comedy a little blacker.*
>
>　　　　　　　　　　　—*The Listener* (1963)

This quotation from *The Listener*, a British arts review, is cited by the *OED* as one of the early uses in the language of *black comedy*, a kind of theatrical counterpart of the BLACK MASS described earlier. Black comedy, also called *black humor*, pokes fun at what generally would be considered pitiable or tragic aspects of the human condition. The term is a direct translation of the French *pièce noire*, and indeed, farcical treatment of violent or tragic subjects was popular in the French theater in the decades following World War II.

Black humor persists today, despite the critics who deplore it as tasteless, but more often in cartoons and skits presented by comedians than as an entire play.

True Blue

Traditionally blue is the color of constancy and faith, the color painters used for the Virgin Mary's robe, the color of the heavens and the oceans. The *OED* even defines blue as "the color of sky and deep sea cerulean."

At the same time, blue has been associated with some less appealing concepts. The early Britons and the modern Maori both tattooed themselves in blue, which they considered a sacrificial color. The Britons went further and used a blue paint (called *woad*) as war paint, since going to war was interpreted as sacrificing oneself. And today a *blue film* is an indecent movie, and a *blue joke* an obscene one.

The word "blue," from Middle English *blew* and Old English *bláw*, has been used since about 1300 to describe a color of the spectrum as well as of the sky and sea. In nineteenth-century America it also acquired the meaning of "sadness," and in 1864 it was defined in J. C. Hotten's *Slang Dictionary* as a word for "indecent." In the twentieth century it also became a commercial symbol for the male sex (along with pink for the female), blue being designated as "for boys" and pink "for girls."

🔹 *Different Shades of Meaning* 🔹

Time writes no wrinkle on thine azure brow.

—LORD BYRON, *Childe Harold's Pilgrimage*

In heraldry blue is called *azure* and signifies chastity, loyalty, and fidelity. Today "azure" is principally a poetic word for blue.

Another name used for blue is, somewhat confusingly, *indigo*. Since the late sixteenth century, this has been the name for a blue dye obtained from a plant that also is called "indigo." Then, in 1704, Sir Isaac Newton used the name "indigo" for one of the seven colors of the spectrum, between blue and violet. It is a dark color, a deep violet-blue or dark gray-blue. Nevertheless, the name continued to be used interchangeably with blue, as in Thomas Carlyle's *Past and Present* (1843), "The sunny plains and deep indigo transparent skies of Italy." And in the twentieth century it sometimes has been used more loosely still. For example, it refers to both the musical genre of *blues* and *blue* in the meaning of "sad" in the popular song *Mood Indigo* (1931), one of Duke Ellington's first big hits. (Written by Irving Mills, Albany Bigard, and Duke Ellington, it originally was an instrumental piece called *Dreamy Blues* but acquired a change of title and lyrics a year after its introduction.)

> *Roses are red, violets are blue,*
> *Sugar is sweet, and so are you.*

The above-quoted children's verse is also somewhat confusing. It probably came originally from Edmund Spenser's *The Faerie Queene* (1596):

> *Roses red and violets blew,*
> *And all the sweetest flowres, that in the forrest*
> *grew.*

However, today we generally call the color of violets "violet" or "purple" rather than "blue," unless, of course, they happen to be white or some other special variety. Poets, on the other hand, take advantage of their license and are less discriminating in this respect, at least with regard to violets. John Keats's sonnet on the color blue calls it "the life of heaven," "the life of waters," and then:

> *Blue! Gentle cousin of the forest-green,*
> *Married to green in all the sweetest flowers—*
> *Forget-me-not,—the Blue bell,—and, that Queen*
> *Of secrecy, the Violet: . . .*

🙠 *Bitten by the Bluetail Fly* 🙠

Like black, blue is a common descriptive part of the names of many plants and animals. In accuracy this usage ranges from considerably so in the case of the *bluet, bluebonnet, blueberry, bluebird*, and *blue jay*, to loose or downright fanciful in the case of the *bluebottle* and the *blue whale*.

The last-named animal is the largest of all surviving animals. It is up to 100 feet long and may weigh as much as 160 tons. Despite its enormous size, it is not particularly threatening, at least not to human beings. Instead of teeth it has a baleen, a structure of horny plates that act as a kind of strainer. Swimming with its mouth wide open, it takes in tons of plankton, krill (tiny shrimplike creatures), and other minute marine animals. Periodically it closes its mouth, strains the water out through the baleen, and swallows the mass of food. As for color, the furrowed skin of the blue whale is more slate-colored than blue, mottled with lighter spots.

In contrast, the *bluetail fly* of the folk song is not even a proper species, although its name may have been based on one—the *bluebottle fly*, a name used for several species with an iridescent blue body. The song, written by Dan Emmett in 1846, became a favorite in American minstrel shows, an extremely popular form of entertainment. It combines the refrain of what was probably an authentic black slave song, "Jimmie crack corn and I don't care," with ballad verses that tell the story of a slave and his happy-go-lucky reaction to his master's death, caused by the bite of a bluetail fly.

Bluebottle is also a common name for various blue flowers, notably the cornflower or bachelor's button, as well as a British nickname for anyone in blue uniform, ranging from a beadle (denounced in Shakespeare's *Henry IV*, Part 2, as "a blue-bottle rogue") to the modern policeman.

❧ *Blue-feathered Friends* ❧

As gay and cheerful as a bluebird in spring.

—DAVY CROCKETT,
Col. Crockett's Exploits and Adventures in Texas (1838)

The *blue jay* is the common crested jay of the American Northeast and has been so called since the early eighteenth century. Common enough to be considered a nuisance, this noisy bird with its bright blue back was regarded as a trickster by some Indian tribes, who ascribed various creative deeds and misdeeds to it.

The *bluebird*, on the other hand, is a much smaller, more attractive songbird, several species of which are found throughout North America. Through a very popular play by the Belgian playwright Maurice Maeterlinck, *L'Oiseau bleu* (French for "bluebird"), it also has become a symbol for happiness, sometimes described as *the bluebird of happiness*. The play, which was first produced in 1908 and appeared in London in English translation in 1910, is basically a fable for children that denies the reality of death; the main characters are a boy and a girl in search of the bluebird.

🙚 *Blue Skies* 🙚

Blue skies, smiling on me,
Nothing but blue skies do I see.

—IRVING BERLIN,
Blue Skies (1927)

A *blue sky* and a *blue day* generally betoken clear weather. "So here has been dawning another blue day," wrote Thomas Carlyle in his essay *Today* (1843). *The blue*, on the other hand, simply means the sky. "How sweet to be a Cloud, floating in the Blue," sings Pooh, A. A. Milne's famous bear. Sometimes this locution is elaborated, as in the U.S. Air Force anthem, "Off we go into the *wide blue yonder*," but more often it is just "the blue," plain and simple.

Occasionally the term is used metaphorically for the sky as the great, vast unknown. Thus we have *vanished into the blue*, meaning a mysterious disappearance to one knows not where, as well as *out of the blue*, meaning an equally mysterious arrival. "I got an encouragement out of the blue," wrote jurist Oliver Wendell Holmes in a letter of 1910. We know he received it unexpectedly, without warning, although presumably he knew its source.

Even greater surprise is signified by *a bolt from the blue*, which likens an unexpected arrival to a bolt of lightning. An early use of this locution occurs in Thomas Carlyle's *History of the French Revolution* (1837): "Arrestment, sudden really as a bolt out of the Blue, has hit strange victims."

Lightning is also the basis of the metaphor *a blue streak*, used to describe something that resembles lightning in both speed and vividness. An American colloquialism dating from the 1820s, it is frequently used to describe a constant stream of words ("She talked a blue streak") or some other rapid movement ("He ran off like a blue streak").

❧ *Once in a Blue Moon* ❧

A *blue moon* has been used as a simile for a very rare occurrence since the early nineteenth century. In fact, however, a blue moon occurs approximately every thirty-two months, because what this term really means is the occurrence of a second full moon in a single month. A full moon comes every 29½ days, when the earth's natural satellite is opposite the sun in the sky. Thus any month except February could see two full moons. Moreover, whenever weather conditions are right, the moon can appear blue in color, regardless of what phase it is in.

Astrologers and other believers in mystical matters hold that a blue moon has a special effect on human affairs. The alignment of earth, moon, and sun do mean the occurrence of stronger tides, but it is questionable whether that lineup of heavenly bodies exerts any special pull on people. Lorenz Hart and Richard Rodgers may well have benefited from any such superstitions. Their song *Blue Moon* (1934), a rewrite of several less successful versions and titles, became one of their first great hits, and a long-lasting one as well. Elvis Presley's 1961 recording of it sold more than a million discs.

❧ *Blue Monday* ❧

Although the word "Monday" is derived from the Old English word for "moon," the moon has nothing whatever to do with *blue Monday*, an expression whose source and meaning have given rise to numerous theories. The term has been around since the Middle Ages, when it signified the Monday before Lent. Some speculate that the "blue" refers to the color used for church decorations on that day. Others hold that this invariably was a day spent in dissipation before the Lenten season imposed austerity, making those who overindulged "blue," meaning "drunk." Still others agree but hold that "blue" rather refers to the uncomfortable feeling of a hangover. The Morrises' *Dictionary of Word and Phrase Origins* proposes another origin. In the days of sailing ships, Monday was the day for flogging miscreants until they were black and blue. More likely, however, the term simply alludes to the fact that Monday is a workday (and schoolday) following a day (or weekend) of pleasure and consequently is depressing.

Largely forgotten is George Gershwin's one-act opera *Blue Monday* (1922), the youthful composer's earliest attempt at a serious work. With a libretto and lyrics by B. G. DeSylva, it was subtitled *Opera Ala Afro-American* and received a single performance on Broadway in 1922 by a white cast in blackface. It was so poorly received that it was cut from the larger show it was in. Although it was later revised and revived several times, Gershwin himself chose to forget both the opera and its title song, *Blue Monday Blues*.

One musician who did not forget it, however, was bandleader Paul Whiteman, who was so impressed with Gershwin's work that he persuaded him to compose a "jazz concerto." In fact, Whiteman announced the "commission" in a newspaper advertisement before even consulting Gershwin but managed to convince the young man to undertake it. The result was Gershwin's best-known serious work, *Rhapsody in Blue* (1924), written for two pianos by Gershwin, orchestrated by Ferde Grofé, and titled by Gershwin's brother Ira.

〜 *Feeling Blue* 〜

> *It's true my butcher's bill is due;*
> *It's true my prospects all look blue.*
>
> —W. S. GILBERT,
> *Bab Ballads* (1869)

To *feel blue* has meant to feel melancholy and *the blues* has meant depression since the eighteenth century or even earlier. Louisa May Alcott had the first term in *Little Women* (1848), "I felt a trifle blue," and the *OED* cites a letter written by actor David Garrick in 1741 that used the second, "I am far from . . . well, tho not troubled with the Blews as I have been."

Much earlier, from the sixteenth century on, to *look blue* meant to be affected with fear or dismay, but this usage is obsolete. Gilbert's meaning in the poem above is the current one—that is, prospects that look blue signify a pessimistic or dreary outlook.

Another term no longer heard very often is *blue devils*, used in the singular in the seventeenth century for a baleful demon and figuratively (in the plural) from the late eighteenth century on for melancholy.

A still current expression of negative emotions is *a blue funk*, which is used in two ways, to mean either extreme fear or agitation or mental depression. The former appears in an 1861 article in *Saturday Review*, "We encounter ... the miserable Dr. Blanding in what is called ... a blue funk" (cited by the *OED*).

🙿 *Blue Notes* 🙿

The distinctive and influential form of black American folk music called *blues* takes its name from one of its features, the frequent occurrence of *blue notes*. A blue note is a half-flatted note, most often on the third or seventh degree of the scale. Basically it is a note that is off pitch—that is, it falls somewhere between two scale notes. The use of such notes gives an effect of wavering between the major and minor modes.

The practice of blue notes probably came from the performance style of folk singers who did not sing according to the conventional rules of tonality. Blues began as a vocal form, but by the early 1900s it was adopted by instrumentalists. The earliest published blues that are still performed are Jelly Roll Morton's *Jelly Roll Blues* (1905) and W. C. Handy's *Memphis Blues* (1912). During the next sixty years the blues influenced nearly every style of popular music—from jazz to rock—as well as many classical composers.

🙿 *Bluegrass* 🙿

Kentucky is known as *the Bluegrass State* because it is so hospitable to that variety of grass, called *Poa pratensis* by the botanist. It is a lush form of ground cover and has been known by that common name since the late eighteenth century. A real-estate advertisement in the *Maryland Journal* on August 17, 1784, read, "This land lies open to the barrens, where there are many hundred acres without timber, and thick set with blue grass." Visitors to Kentucky admired its grassy plains, but many of them, including John Ciardi, claim they have seen only green grass there—a bluish-green, perhaps, but definitely green.

Nevertheless, the name sticks and also was applied to a kind of country music originating in Kentucky. *Bluegrass music* features a fast, two-beat style, and the basic instruments used to perform it are the banjo, fiddle, mandolin, and guitar. The vocal part is characteristic of earlier mountain ballads, with one voice singing well above the melody, almost falsetto. Chief among the early performers who popularized this style over the radio and through recordings were Bill Monroe and his Blue Grass Boys, active in the 1930s. During the next half century bluegrass music became big business, a staple product of country music.

❧ *Blue as . . .* ❧

And everyone on board ship looked as blue as blazes.

> —SAMUEL A. HAMMETT,
> *Piney Woods Tavern* (1858)

Blue as an indigo bag (1834) and *blue as larkspur* are self-explanatory similes, as are *blue as the sky, blue as a violet* (given poetic license, as discussed above), and *blue as steel* (similarly stretching the point a little, as Herman Melville did in *Moby Dick* in 1851). More puzzling are *blue as a razor*, which in the 1860s meant being either in high feather or dead drunk, and *blue as an old maid*, which meant extremely moral and upright and prudish. Happily these last two similes appear to be obsolete.

More understandable than these was the contemporary *blue as brimstone*, which no doubt alludes to the bluish look of a pale flame. To *burn blue*, meaning a pale flame without a red glare, was already known to Shakespeare, who used the term in *Richard III*: "The lights burne blew" (5:3).

Which takes us back to *blue as blazes*, presumably again alluding to a blue flame. And then there is just plain *blue blazes*, which the above-quoted Samuel Hammett also used in the same account, saying, "Cold as blue blazes," and elsewhere, "swore like blue blazes." Further, a quarter of a century earlier, John Neal had written, "Hot as blue blazes" (*The Down-Easters*, 1833). Perhaps we must conclude that the same "blue blazes" simply was a colorful simile for "very" or "extremely," which is how it is used today.

&. *The Ever-Loving Blue-eyed World* &.

She blued—and almost starched and ironed him—with her cobalt eyes.

—O. HENRY, *To Him Who Waits* (1909)

Cartoonist Walt Kelly, word-player par excellence and creator of Pogo, often embroidered stock phrases. Thus "what in the world" became "what in the ever-loving blue-eyed world." The "blue-eyed world" was essentially what his kindly opossum, Pogo, thought of it—that is, a basically good place. For centuries, *blue-eyed* has betokened beauty and goodness, much like the "fair-haired" with which it often keeps company. And in O. Henry's story, it is the power of those blue eyes (cobalt being another synonym for "blue") that he is describing, however ironic his allusion to laundry bluing.

Homer had another association with blue eyes. His *blue-eyed maid* was Athena, the goddess of wisdom. About the seventeenth century this expression underwent a sex change and became the *blue-eyed boy*, meaning at first merely innocent and ingenuous, but soon acquiring the additional connotation of the favorite. The last is what is generally meant by the expression today. It was so used by P. G. Wodehouse in *Bill the Conqueror* (1924), "If ever there was a blue-eyed boy, you will be it."

A far newer phenomenon is the *blue-haired lady*. The practice of using blue rinses to prevent white hair from taking on an unattractive yellowish tinge became prevalent in the 1930s. A couple of decades later the practice was so closely associated with a conventional middle-class woman of a certain age that the term became a general descriptive one for this type of person.

Blue eyes can be acquired by means of tinted contact lenses and blue hair with a rinse. But blue is also used to describe some physical conditions that would be harder to fake, as it were, even if they were desirable. Turning *blue with cold*, for example, would not be readily done. But in fact extreme cold does give both the lips and extremities a bluish cast. Nietzsche described it in *Thus Spake Zarathustra* (trans. 1909), "Winter, a bad guest, sitteth with me at home; blue are my hands with his friendly handshaking."

It is but a short step from blue with cold to blue with death. "How wonderful is Death . . . with lips of lurid blue," wrote Shelley (*The Daemon of the World*, 1816). The connection survives in the term *blue baby* for an infant with congenital cyanosis; this term first was cited in a medical text in 1903.

Turning *blue in the face*, on the other hand, is far less serious. This description for being breathless and exhausted from having made a great effort dates from the nineteenth century. Anthony Trollope uses it in *The Small House at Allington* (1864): "You may talk to her till you're both blue in the face."

Or you might scream *blue murder*. Violent death doesn't enter into this expression, which merely indicates extreme vexation or, sometimes, alarm. Rather, it is a corruption of the French *morbleu*, signifying much the same thing. It in turn is a contraction of *mort de dieu*, literally "God's death," but serving simply as an expletive.

Yet another blue body part is the *bluenose*, which has never been used other than figuratively. In early nineteenth-century America it was used for a native of Nova Scotia, a locality known for its production of a purplish potato variety called "bluenose." Indeed, this explanation is spelled out by Thomas Haliburton in one of his *Sam Slick* tales (c. 1837) but has never been verified. Then, either because the Nova Scotians were boastful and snooty about their potatoes or because a blue nose was associated with literal, and hence figurative, coldness, bluenose came to be used, from the 1860s on, for an excessively priggish and puritanical person. This last meaning is the one that remains current.

Last but far from least, we have *blue blood*, which has long signified being of high or noble birth. The term has nothing to do with blood deprived of oxygen. Rather, it is a translation of the Spanish *sangre azul*, which was used to describe Spain's pure-blooded aristocrats, those whose ancestors had not intermarried with the Moors. Consequently such persons were fairly light-skinned, and their veins showed bluer through the skin than Spaniards of mixed blood. The expression was used in Britain from the early nineteenth century on and was, like so many, poked fun at by W. S. Gilbert. When the heroine of his *Iolanthe*, the shepherdess Phyllis, fails to be impressed by Lord Tolloller's title and ancestry, the nobleman complains,

Blue blood! blue blood!
When virtuous love is sought
Thy power is naught,
Though dating from the Flood,
Blue blood!

➜ Boys and Girls in Blue ➜

Little boy blue, come blow your horn.

The familiar nursery rhyme about the shepherd boy who sleeps while the sheep graze in a forbidden meadow dresses him in blue, for no particular reason. The term *boys in blue*, however, has signified since the mid-nineteenth century various male groups who wear blue uniforms: first the police; then sailors; and in the American Civil War, the Union troops (the Confederates wore gray). In Great Britain a sailor was also referred to as a *blue jacket* to distinguish him from a marine.

Another British term is *blue gown*, which signifies a harlot. It comes from the fact that prostitutes thrown in jail used to be made to wear a blue dress to distinguish them from other prisoners. This definitely is *not* the meaning intended in the song *In My Sweet Little Alice Blue Gown* (1919). Joseph McCarthy's lyrics immortalized a light blue color made fashionable by President Theodore Roosevelt's daughter Alice Longworth, who particularly favored it, and the song became one of America's favorite waltzes.

To be called a *bluestocking*, on the other hand, is to receive a sexist insult that originated in the eighteenth century. It comes from an eighteenth-century salon in London where intellectuals met to discuss serious and learned subjects. Modeled after an earlier such salon in Paris, it was founded by a Mrs. Montague about 1750 and was so named because some of its prominent members (male) wore stockings of blue worsted instead of the conventional black silk. However, it is to women that the name "bluestocking" was attached, coming to stand for any intellectual woman who preferred concerning herself with matters of the mind rather than fashion or the "feminine" graces. Although she was not known as an outstanding feminist, Elizabeth Barrett Browning felt strongly enough to protest in her *Aurora Leigh* (1857), "Is the blue in eyes as awful as in stockings?"

~ *Blue-collar Clothes* ~

The term *blue collar*, meaning manual or industrial labor and those employed in it, originated in the United States shortly after World War II. The "blue" may have originally referred to blue denim, long a material for work clothes, but soon was more generally applied to any kind of job requiring special garments.

The most famous item of clothing associated with such work is *blue jeans*, which actually have been made since the mid-nineteenth century. The cloth from which they were made, denim, derives its name from the French *serge de Nîmes*, where it used to be manufactured; the word *jeans* similarly is derived from a place of production, the Italian city of Genoa, where denim used to be woven. Although Herman Melville used the name in his *Israel Potter* of 1855 ("Across the otherwise blue-jean career of Israel, Paul Jones flits and re-flits like a crimson thread"), it was not commonly and exclusively used for overalls and work pants until the 1930s. Nor did it become a worldwide fashion for several decades.

In 1989, according to a *New York Times* article (February 3, 1991), retail sales for blue jeans were six billion dollars, representing one of the largest categories of apparel. And, the report continued, although American domestic demand had suffered from both a recession and the "graying of the jeans generation," foreign demand was still on the rise. Farmers, ranchers, and laborers have always worn blue denim work clothes, but as a fashion for those with whiter collars, blue jeans have been cyclical. They represented social rebellion in the 1960s and entered the realm of high fashion in the early 1980s.

As blue jeans became fashionable, their color range expanded. They became available not only in many different shades of blue but also in black, white, and practically all the colors of the rainbow (and even some absent from it).

❧ *Bluebeard's Castle* ❧

Women rather take to terrible people; prize-fighters, pirates, highwaymen, rebel generals, Grand Turks, and Bluebeards generally have a fascination for the sex.

—OLIVER WENDELL HOLMES,
The Guardian Angel (1867)

Many modern feminists would agree with Holmes's seemingly sexist statement, especially those concerned with the issue of "women who love too much," or women who stay married to abusive husbands. The tale of Bluebeard continues to have relevance in modern times.

Bluebeard, of course, is the title and villain of a widespread folk tale that features a murderous husband and a wife who breaks a taboo (enters a forbidden chamber). In Charles Perrault's fairy tale, Fatima is forbidden to look in one locked room of the castle, but during Bluebeard's absence she obtains the key and looks anyhow. Inside she finds the remains of six of Bluebeard's former wives. She drops the key, which becomes bloodstained.

Bluebeard returns, discovers what she did, and threatens her death, but she is saved by her brothers.

The story, whose ultimate origin is not known, has had wide appeal over the centuries, and today *Bluebeard* still means a man who has murdered one or more of his wives, or other women.

🏕 *Blue Laws* 🏕

Practically every culture abhors and outlaws murder, but *blue laws* are a quite different sort of restriction. The term appears to have originated in late-eighteenth-century America, and its precise source has been lost. The enactment of laws to enforce church rulings on religious observance and morals dates from colonial times. Such laws prohibited, for example, dancing of any kind, drinking or working on Sundays, and the like. The "blue" here means puritanical or morally strict.

Although the days of the Puritans are long since past, many American localities still have blue laws, for the most part regulating the operation of various commercial enterprises on Sundays. The most common extant law prohibits selling liquor on Sunday, at least during the time of the traditional morning church service, contravening the nation's constitutionally protected separation of church and state.

Blue-sky laws, on the other hand, are a different kettle of fish entirely. This term has been used since the early twentieth century for regulations that forbid dealing in worthless or doubtful stocks and bonds. The name is believed to allude to the idea that a clever salesperson can sell anything—even the blue sky—to a credulous buyer.

Unscrupulous stockbrokers rarely deal in *blue-chip* stocks, a name used since the late 1920s for high-value securities of impeccable status. This term comes from several gambling games, including both faro and poker, where chips are used to represent money, and blue-colored ones are the most valuable, often representing ten times the value of the cheapest, which are red.

> *The essence of any blue material is timing. If you*
> *sit on it, it becomes vulgar.*
>
> —Attributed to comedian DANNY LA RUE

The meaning of "blue" in blue laws—that is, puritanical—is exactly the opposite of the "blue" in *blue films* or *blue jokes*, where it signifies "risqué" or indecent. It has been so used since the mid-nineteenth century, and no one is quite sure why. One writer speculates that it comes from a Chinese custom of painting brothels blue on the outside. Another more plausibly suggests that it comes from the use of blue spotlights when strippers go into the gamier part of their act. Some performers, it appears from the quotation above, differentiate between "blue" and downright indecent, but the distinction is by no means universal.

&. *Blue Books* &.

One theory concerning the term "blue laws" is that they were written down in blue-covered books. There is no evidence for this origin, but other kinds of *blue book* have been around since the early seventeenth century. In Britain, the official reports of Parliament and the Privy Council were kept in blue-covered folios from at least 1633 on. In the United States a similar binding was used for a book listing all those who held government office, from 1836 on.

In addition, there are several modern kinds of blue book. An official *Blue Book* lists the current market value of used cars by model and year of manufacture, and the name has been extended to other manuals of market value for a variety of products. And finally, a blue book used in American schools and colleges, and one that tends to arouse extreme anxiety in students, is a blank, blue-covered booklet for writing examinations.

Teachers and professors correcting blue books use just about any kind of pen or pencil. The *blue pencil*, on the other hand, is indelibly associated with editorial corrections, changes, and deletions. It somehow became the custom for editors to mark their emendations with a blue pencil. The term, which became synonymous with editing, began to be so used in the late nineteenth century (it first appeared in print in 1888, according to the *OED*) and has long survived the actual use of blue pencils.

Even in the days of computerized design, however, the traditional *blueprint* survives. This term originated with a late nineteenth-century process of making a photographic print composed of white lines on a blue ground, used for copying architectural plans and the like. From the 1920s on, however, the term also began to be used for any mechanical drawing or similar plan, whatever the color of the paper, as well as figuratively for any detailed outline or plan of action. Both usages remain current.

🐝 *Something Old, Something New* . . . 🐝

"Something borrowed, something blue," continues the old rhyme that specifies what a bride should wear on her wedding day to ensure good fortune. The custom is still followed by many brides, even though its origin has been lost.

Often as not the blue item is a *blue ribbon*, although brides do not necessarily use it for its present meaning

—"of the highest excellence" or "first prize." This usage comes from the wide blue ribbon that is the badge of honor of the Garter, the most coveted British order of knighthood. It was originally founded by King Edward III about 1350 and was reestablished in the nineteenth century. To finance his foreign wars Edward depended heavily on the support of noblemen, whom he then rewarded with this honor. According to popular legend, a lady at a court ball lost her blue garter, which the King picked up. In response to the questioning glances so aroused, he bound the garter around his own leg and said, *Honi soit qui mal y pense* (French for "Shame on him who thinks evil of it"), which became the motto of the Order of the Garter. (The French have a comparable honor, the Order of the Holy Ghost, which became famous for serving fine food at its gatherings, and consequently the name of its award, *cordon bleu*, also meaning "blue ribbon," became attached to elegant cookery.)

Over the years, blue ribbon was extended to mean

anything of superior quality or prominence, as well as the top award in various competitions—for example, a horse show.

🙪 *True Blue* 🙪

"Blue is true," says the old nursery rhyme, echoing an old sentiment. Blue is the color of constancy, and as with similar symbolism there are a number of theories concerning its source. One holds that it refers to the unchanging sky. Another claims that it alludes to the fastness of a blue dye, which unlike others will not run. This theory is upheld by a proverb that appears in several early collections, "True blue will never stain." Still another source holds that the proverb alludes to the wearing of blue aprons by butchers because they do not reveal bloodstains. And in 1662 Thomas Fuller explained that "He is true Coventry blue," meaning he is a loyal friend, alludes to the fact that the best blues were those dyed in the town of Coventry.

In the seventeenth century the Scottish Covenanters, who pledged to uphold Presbyterianism, were called "true blue"; their color was blue, whereas that of the royal side was red. Samuel Butler used this turn of phrase in *Hudibras* (1663): " 'Twas Presbyterian true blue."

Many decades later, when religious strife was no longer a big issue, *true blue* in Britain meant staunchly Tory. Today, however, it is used in a more general sense on both sides of the Atlantic, simply meaning staunchly loyal—to a cause, team, etc.

Brown as a Berry

Although it is abundantly found in nature, brown is not one of the colors of the spectrum. On the painter's palette it is produced by mixing black and orange. The word itself comes from *bruin*, or "bear," and indeed most species of bear are one or another shade of brown. Yet from the first it also meant "dark" or "dusky," a meaning preserved in BROWN STUDY (see below).

In mythology and folklore brown was identified with the earth and autumn, and more figuratively still, with penitence and sorrow. The analogy to dried-up autumnal nature is obvious: "When all the fields are lying brown and bare," wrote the Civil War poet Thomas Buchanan Read in *The Closing Scene*. The transfer to human appearance is also self-evident—weathered and browned by

the sun and wind. Sir Walter Scott used it in *The Lady of the Lake* (1810):

> *What though the sun, with ardent frown,*
> *Had slightly tinged her cheek with brown.*

And, of course, brown also describes a genetically dark skin color, both in a nickname such as the BROWN BOMBER (see below) and in George Bush's campaign euphemism for his Mexican-American grandchildren, LITTLE BROWN ONES (see below).

> *We walke in the Sun . . . but our faces are tanned*
> *before we return.*
>
> —STEPHEN GOSSON,
> *The School of Abuse* (1579)

Two terms for *light brown* are in common use: *beige* and *tan*. The first, describing a grayish light brown, comes from the Old French *bege*, itself of uncertain origin. The second, used more for a yellowish light brown, comes from the Middle English *tannen*, meaning to tan—that is, make a hide into leather by soaking it with tanbark (from oak or another kind of tree), whose active ingredient is *tannic acid*.

By the sixteenth century the verb forms of *tan* widely meant the darkening of skin by exposure to sun. Until the twentieth century this was considered a blemish rather than a mark of health and beauty, a view again becoming prominent with the discovery that such exposure is a major cause of skin cancer. Nevertheless, today we have *tanning parlors* that expose people to artificial sunlight as well as many kinds of *suntan lotion* and *sunscreen* to protect the skin against overexposure.

❧ *Brown as a Berry* ❧

One of the earliest similes involving brown is also a puzzling one. Chaucer used it in the Prologue to his *Canterbury Tales* (c. 1390)—"His palfrey [horse] was as broune as is a berry"—as well as in *The Coke's Tale*. The comparison has survived for more than six centuries despite the fact that few, if any, berries in nature are actually brown. Robert Louis Stevenson elaborated somewhat in a letter of 1874, "Brown as a berry with sun." Unpicked, sun-dried berries often do dry up and turn brown, and this piece of logic is preserved in the present-day use of the simile for those whose skin has turned brown in the sun ("He's been outside all day and is brown as a berry").

A few other similes recur, although with less frequency. *Brown as a chestnut* and *brown as mahogany* both date from the first half of the nineteenth century. *Brown as a nut*, more often in the form of *nut-brown*, is much older. John Milton used it in *L'Allegro* (c. 1630), "Then to the spicy nut-brown ale." *Brown as coffee* presumably followed by some decades the introduction of this beverage to America and Europe in the mid-seventeenth century, but despite the continued popularity of coffee this expression is rarely heard nowadays.

One last simile, *brown as leather*, brings to mind the shade of light brown called TAN (see above). Helen Gray Cone (1859–1934) used it in her poem *Greencastle Jenny*:

Pickett's Virginians were passing through,
Supple as steel and brown as leather.

🍂 *How Now, Brown Cow?* 🍂

One of the principal breeds of dairy cattle is the *Brown Swiss*, which is largely brown in color and was originally bred in Switzerland. Valuable beasts, they are rugged, thrive well on rough pasturelands, and have an unusually long milk-producing season. It is doubtful, however, that *how now, brown cow* refers to this breed. In the early eighteenth century *brown cow* was a humorous name for a barrel of beer, but this phrase, whose source has been lost, may come from an elocution lesson for teaching correct vowel pronunciation.

Numerous birds have brown in their coloration, but even when that color predominates it is not part of their name. A major exception is the *brown thrasher*, which American bird expert Roger Tory Peterson describes as "rufous," meaning reddish-brown. And indeed that is part of its Latin name, *Toxostoma rufum rufum*. A close relative of the catbird and mockingbird, the brown thrasher is fairly large, about ten to twelve inches long, and except for two light-colored wing bars and a striped underside, is entirely brown. It breeds in thickets and shrubbery and is found throughout the eastern half of North America, from Canada to the Gulf of Mexico. It is the state bird of Georgia.

In contrast to this native American bird, the *brown trout* (*Salmo trutta*) was introduced to North America from Europe and has managed to establish itself in many areas. It thrives in warmer waters than the brook trout and has replaced native fishes in many of the streams in which it is found. With its yellowish-brown sides marked with reddish spots, it is hardly a pure brown but comes about as close to it as any fish.

Health Food

In the past couple of decades, the increasing emphasis on "natural" or "health" foods led to a large-scale commercial reversal. Instead of finding new ways to *refine* foods, companies now stressed the so-called natural and unrefined. There was a resurgence in sales of *brown sugar*, which is either unrefined or only partly refined, and therefore touted as "more nutritious" than white sugar. The same was true of *brown rice*—unpolished rice in which the germ and yellow outer layer containing bran are retained and that actually does have more nutritive value than white rice.

There also was a revival of *brown bread*, as any bread of dark color has been known since the late fifteenth century. Matthew Henry (1662–1714) mentioned it in his Biblical *Commentaries*: "It was a common saying among the Puritans, 'Brown bread and the Gospel is good fare.' "

In keeping with this blessing, brown bread came to the New World with the Pilgrims and Puritans. New England in particular became famous for a variety called *Boston brown bread*. Its basic ingredients are rye flour, corn flour, molasses, and sour milk; sometimes raisins or dates are added. Unlike baked breads, it is steamed in a mold—that is, the mold is put on a rack inside a kettle of boiling water, with the water coming halfway up the mold's sides. It is cooked for three hours or longer.

According to Imogene Wolcott's *Yankee Cookbook*, the classic baked brown bread had a crust so thick and tough that it was cut off and never eaten, but saved until the next baking day. It then was softened in water and stirred into the new batter to give the bread a rich, dark brown color. Some families even held that their brown bread was "primeval" because each batch contained remnants of a former baking and the original bread dated back so far that no one could remember when it had been baked.

Well into the twentieth century, the traditional New England Saturday night supper menu consisted of baked beans and brown bread. William Cowper Brann (1855–1898), a journalist who was called the Iconoclast from the name of his Texas newspaper (and who was shot by an outraged reader), wrote, "Boston runs to brain as well as to beans and brown bread."

The only thing Boston brown bread has in common with today's *brown-and-serve* bakery goods is the word "brown." The latter, a convenience food invented after World War II, requires only a few minutes in a hot oven before being deemed ready to eat. Although ads claim it tastes just like the home-baked product, the difference is considerable.

Another American delicacy dating from colonial times is *brown betty*, a baked pudding consisting of apple slices covered with sugar (and/or molasses), nutmeg, cinnamon, and flour or bread crumbs, and topped with bits of butter. An 1864 issue of the *Yale Literary Magazine* made the harsh announcement that for athletes in training, "tea, coffee, pies, and 'brown Betty' must next be sacrificed."

The apples in brown betty might help persuade a willing believer that this dessert is a health food, but that rationalization could scarcely hold for another American sweet, the *brownie*. It is a small, brown, cakelike square made with chocolate and, usually, chopped nuts, and its name dates from the late nineteenth century. In print, the term appeared in a Sears, Roebuck catalog of 1897.

In Britain, on the other hand, brownie is a name for a benevolent goblin, so called since the early sixteenth century because it usually wears a hooded brown cloak. It does useful work during the night, but if its labors are criticized it will do mischief, such as breaking dishes or spilling milk. Originating in Scottish folklore (England's equivalent spirit is also called Robin Goodfellow), the brownie is a rural creature, haunting farms more than city dwellings. To get rid of it one must make it a new little cloak and hood.

🍂 *Brownie Points* 🍂

Since 1916 the youngest group of Girl Guides, ranging in age from seven to eleven, has been known as the Brownies. And since 1916 the name has been used for members aged seven to nine in their American counterpart, the Girl Scouts. Like the other members of these organizations dedicated to fostering good citizenship and service, the Brownies earn "points" when they attain certain levels of achievement or perform various services; the points eventually are translated into awards. By the mid-twentieth century *brownie points* had been transferred to general usage to mean credit for doing the right thing in any endeavor. For example, it might be said that "Ms. Jones earned quite a few brownie points for writing that ten-page report for her boss."

Finally, *brownie* has had one other meaning that, however, has become virtually obsolete. In the early twentieth century Kodak used it, capitalized, as the trade name for a small, simple camera, which came on the market in 1902. It was housed in a brown case, which no doubt was the source of its name. A simple instrument, it was a first camera for many children (this writer found it under her Christmas tree about 1940) as well as for such great photographers as Ansel Adams, but it has long since been replaced by more sophisticated models.

The name *brown goods*, however, is a newer one (used

from the 1970s or so) for products that often are made in a brown case, particularly appliances such as television sets, radios, and the like (as opposed to appliances usually encased in white, such as washing machines and refrigerators).

❧ *Brown Study* ❧

> *It seems to me (said she) that you are in some brown study.*

> —JOHN LYLY, *Euphues* (1579)

Back in the fourteenth century, to be "in a study" meant to be lost in thought. In the sixteenth century, this phrase was elaborated with the addition of "brown." Etymologists suggest that the reason lies in the archaic sense of brown as "dusky" or "dark," but this does not make a great deal more sense than considering brown purely a color. Nevertheless, the locution persisted, from the 1500s into the present century.

Furthermore, lexicographers also disagree as to the term's exact meaning. Some hold that it means being deeply contemplative of some quite serious matter; others maintain it means to be absentminded, seemingly engrossed in deep thought but actually merely daydreaming.

> *Little I ask; my wants are few,*
> *I only wish a hut of stone*
> *(A* very plain *brownstone will do)*
> *That I may call my own.*

> —OLIVER WENDELL HOLMES,
> *Contentment* (1858)

Perhaps Holmes was in a brown study when he mused upon a hut of his own. Interestingly enough, this Brahmin poet, of wealthy New England stock, picked as his example of the plain and simple a *brownstone*, which by the mid-nineteenth century invoked visions of upper-class society in America.

Brownstone is simply a brownish-red sandstone used as a building material. It is employed particularly for the facades of houses, and houses so faced are called "brownstones." But in the nineteenth century houses of this kind were built mainly in the form of town houses for the well-to-do in American cities, and for a time the name became synonymous with this social class. Today, although the word mainly signifies a type of building, well-preserved examples of brownstones in cities such as Boston and New York are still highly regarded and command a premium price.

🕮 *In a Plain Brown Wrapper* 🕮

The term *brown paper* has been used for coarse wrapping paper since the sixteenth century. To risk stating the very obvious, fashions for what is appropriate change. In the first half of the twentieth century, reading matter of a dubious or prurient nature—pornographic books, for example—were often enclosed in *plain brown wrapping paper* (by the publisher, shipper, reader, or all three) to camouflage them. The very presence of a plain brown wrapper, therefore, implied such concealment.

Today this practice is more or less obsolete, at least in most places, where one can find sex magazines openly displayed at any newsstand. However, the plain brown wrapper is finding new life in a time of heightened environmentalist consciousness. Perfectly respectable periodicals such as *The New Yorker* have taken to enclosing mailed copies in biodegradable protective brown paper, which replaced their ecologically undesirable polyethylene wrappers.

With similar concern, some American communities with a mandatory recycling program insist that discarded newspapers be packed in brown paper bags of the kind widely used in grocery stores. However, decades before this practice began, the term *to brown-bag* was being used to mean bringing one's lunch to work in a bag, or, alternatively, to bring along an alcoholic beverage when patronizing a restaurant without a liquor license. The lunch-carrier in particular was called a *brown-bagger*, regardless of whether the food was actually carried in a brown paper bag. The liquor-carrier might be practicing some concealment, like the above-described brown wrapper, in contravention of local laws, but not necessarily so.

In Great Britain, on the other hand, the term had a quite different meaning. There a brown bagger was, as defined in a 1930 school magazine, what American students derided as a "grind" or a "nerd"—an excessively diligent student who devotes his or her entire time to studying and never engages in any social or frivolous pursuits. This name apparently referred to the brown schoolbag or attaché case such individuals frequently carried.

❧ Do It Up Brown ❧

To do it up brown has meant, since the mid-nineteenth century, to do something thoroughly. The estimable Eric Partridge believed the term may have originally alluded to John Brown's famous raid on Harper's Ferry, Virginia, in 1859, but this theory is clearly mistaken, since there are earlier references to it in print. More likely the expression alludes to something being thoroughly cooked or roasted, and therefore well browned.

A very similar expression, which is no longer heard much in America but apparently survives in Britain, is *to do someone brown*, which means to trick, deceive, or cheat someone. James Russell Lowell had it in *Bigelow Papers* (1848): "Her own representatives do her quite brown." This, too, may come from cookery, analogous to the current usage of "to roast" as meaning to ridicule or criticize.

> *What the hell had he got to be so browned off about?*
>
> —J. CURTIS, *They Drive By Night* (1938)

The slang use of *browned off* for angry or disgusted comes from the first half of the twentieth century. Eric Partridge held it was Regular Army slang dating from World War I, but the earliest citation in the *OED* is 1938.

By World War II the far less polite *brown-nose* was widely used in the U.S. armed services and fairly soon crossed the Atlantic. This still current slang term for sycophancy refers, of course, to ass-kissing and graphically depicts the result if said backside is less than clean.

Two other terms date from this period. *Brown Shirt*, a name for members of Hitler's Nazi Party, appears in English from the early 1930s on. *Brownout* is of slightly later provenance. After the start of World War II, it was used in Australia and the United States for a partial blackout—the reduction or elimination of night lighting in cities—as a precaution against air raids. Later it also was extended to mean a curtailment of electric power resulting from a violent storm, overtaxed power facilities, or the like.

Lo, with a band of bowmen and of pikes,
Brown bills and targetiers.

—CHRISTOPHER MARLOWE,
Edward II (1594)

In contrast, two terms from much earlier warfare, the
brown Bill and *brown Bess*, are obsolete. The first, a nickname for the foot soldier's halberd, probably derived from
the fact that it was usually brown with rust (although
some authorities feel the "brown" may have referred to
the fact that it was burnished, or shiny). The name was
used for both the weapon and the soldiers themselves, as
in Marlowe's play.

Brown Bess was the British Army nickname for an
eighteenth-century flintlock musket and probably alluded to the color of its wooden stock, usually made of
walnut. The term appeared in print from the beginning
of the eighteenth century but disappeared along with the
weapon.

In the modern martial arts of judo and karate, a
brown belt signifies an intermediate level of expertise,
approximately halfway between the beginner's white belt
and the top-ranking expert's black belt. The term has
been so used in English since the late 1930s.

❧ *The Brown Bomber* ❧

One of the first black athletes to achieve worldwide fame
was boxer Joe Louis, whom the press nicknamed *the
Brown Bomber*—brown for his skin color and bomber for
the power of his punches. Born Joseph Louis Barrow in
1914, he was heavyweight boxing champion of the world
longer than anyone else in boxing history, from 1937 to
1949. During this period he defended his crown twenty-
five times; of his seventy-one professional fights, he lost

only three. Louis's first defeat was a surprising setback
by the German boxer Max Schmeling, but in his next
bout against him, in 1938, he knocked out Schmeling in
the first round.

During World War II Louis served in the U.S. Army
and fought a number of times in charity exhibition
matches. He retired in 1949, undefeated as champion. A
few years later, in need of money, he came out of retire-
ment, but although winning some bouts, he never re-
gained the championship and soon afterward ended his
career.

And so from these brown-handed children
Shall grow mighty rulers of state.

—Mary Hannah Krout (1857–1927),
Little Brown Hands

Although today the word "black" is used far more often
than "brown" to describe dark-colored skin, in the nineteenth century *brown* was used in the sense of mulatto.
President George Bush revived this usage during his
Presidential campaign in 1988. Probably to broaden his
appeal to nonwhite voters and indicate his lack of racial
and ethnic prejudice, he referred to grandchildren of his
as *little brown ones*; specifically, these were the children
of Bush's son and his Mexican wife.

Gray Eminence

*A*n indeterminate sort of color, gray is more or less halfway between black and white, the color of ash or lead. The word comes from the Old English *græg* and is often spelled *grey* in Great Britain, Australia, and other English-speaking countries.

"Grey is a colour that always seems on the eve of changing to some other colour," wrote G. K. Chesterton (in *Alarms and Discursions*, 1910). Indeed, its very indefiniteness has made the word a synonym for vagueness. We speak of *a gray area* between, for example, legal and illegal, truth and falsehood, good and bad, and a host of other issues that cannot be clearly categorized.

When all candels be out, all cats be grey.

—JOHN HEYWOOD,
English Proverbs (1546)

Versions of this proverb recorded by Heywood have been repeated over and over, by writers as diverse as Cervantes and Tobias Smollett, and in French, German, and other languages as well. In the dark one can't distinguish one kind or color from another, they might have said, but *gray* is what they picked to mean "indistinguishable." A similar usage appeared in a *New York Times* music review in 1990: "Mr. Goode, his mane now prematurely silver, is anything but a gray performer. He commands, in fact, a wider spectrum of tone color than any pianist of his generation" (see also TONE COLOR).

In folklore, gray symbolizes barrenness, concealment, and discretion, as well as sadness, grief, and renunciation. We speak of an overcast or cloudy day as a *gray day*, one that many individuals find depressing. Shakespeare wrote of the *gray of the morning*, meaning the subdued light of dawn, and Byron wrote of the *gray of twilight*, at nightfall.

❧ *As Grey as Grannum's Cat* ❧

"As grey as Grannum's cat," wrote Thomas Fuller in his compendium *Gnomologia* (1732), and this simile was still current in the late nineteenth century. However, numerous other comparisons involving gray are both older and more commonly used.

Chaucer wrote of eyes as *gray as a falcon* (in his translation of the *Roman de la Rose*), *gray as glass* (in the Prologue to *Canterbury Tales*), and *gray as a goose* (in the *Miller's Tale*). Another popular simile is *gray as a badger*. Jonathan Swift used it about 1720: "Though she lives till she's as grey as a badger all over" (*Works*), here meaning until she is silvered with age. Badgers are not gray all over—indeed, their name comes from the white blaze most species have on their foreheads—but they have grizzled fur, very similar to the hair of dark-haired human beings whose hair is turning gray.

Badgers are less widespread in the United States than in England. From America come the expressions *gray as a fox* and *gray as an opossum*, both from the first half of the nineteenth century. Further, there are *gray as a rat* and *gray as steel*, the latter used by Herman Melville in the mid-nineteenth century (and today we often use *steel-gray* for a shade resembling the color of that metal).

Although nature abounds with gray-colored animals, ranging from cats to elephants to the common *gray squirrel* (*Sciurus carolinensis* to zoologists), few of them figure in such similes. Some, however, are linguistically preserved in other ways.

? *The Old Gray Mare* ?&

The old gray mare,
she ain't what she used to be.

— American folk song

The gray mare has figured in song and story for centuries. John Heywood's proverb collection of 1546 has, "The grey mare is the better horse," an idea that some believe is derived from a preference for the gray mares of Flanders over the finest English coach horses. Whether or not this is the origin, the proverb not only survived but also came to mean that the wife (mare being a female) rules the husband. This idea became so well known that the term *gray mare* alone came to express the entire thought.

My papa he keeps three horses,
Black, and white, and dapple grey, sir.

—W. S. GILBERT, *The Gondoliers* (1889)

In the days of the horse-drawn coach, gray horses were considered quite elegant, especially when they were a matched pair. In those days, *the gray* often meant a gray horse, and *grays* a pair of them. It is spelled out in Mrs. C. Gildersleeve's humorous poem *Mrs. Lofty and I* (c. 1885):

> *Mrs. Lofty keeps a carriage,*
> > *So do I;*
> *She has dappled grays to draw it,*
> > *None have I.*

& *Gray Goose* &

> *Gray goose and gander,*
> *Waft your wings together.*

> —Nursery rhyme

The common European wild goose (*Anser anser*), from which most domestic geese have been developed, was known simply as a *gray goose* from about the year 1000. (Since the early seventeenth century it also has been known as *graylag*, a name thought to come from the fact that it was the last of the wild geese to migrate south in winter—that is, it lagged behind other species.)

Apart from figuring in nursery rhymes and folklore, the gray goose became the subject of an American Negro ballad that originated in the days of slavery and was preserved as a work song by black convicts in the Texas State Penitentiary. (It was heard there by John A. and Alan Lomax, who recorded it in their famous folk song collection.) In the ballad *The Gray Goose*, the goose survives being shot by a hunter, being plucked, and being cooked, and then is still too tough to eat. Sent to a sawmill, it breaks the saw's teeth and finally flies off across the ocean with "a long string of goslin's" behind it. In other words, no matter how you punish the goose, it will always survive, just as the black will survive imprisonment and other punishment and will walk away laughing.

❧ *Greyhounds* ❧

A gentleman's greyhound and a saltbox, seek them at the fire.

—EDWARD HERBERT, *Jacula Prudentum* (1640)

The greyhound, whose lineage can be traced to ancient Egypt, has long been valued for hunting, which it does entirely by sight rather than scent, and for its speed. Its eagerness to go was documented by Shakespeare: "I see you stand like greyhounds in the slips, straining upon the start" (*Henry V*, 3:1). Since the early twentieth century, greyhounds, named for their silky gray hair, have been trained for racing—a dummy hare is mechanically propelled around a track and is pursued by greyhounds. By the 1920s this sport was popular enough so that a magazine called *Greyhound Racing* was flourishing.

In the late nineteenth century, when ever-faster steamships were being built, particularly for transatlantic crossings, the name "greyhound" was transferred to the speediest of these ocean liners. By the mid-twentieth century air travel was rapidly replacing ocean voyages, and in America the dog's name was adopted by America's largest intercity bus company, *Greyhound Lines*, which despite its name and claims never became famous for its swiftness. The association survives, however. A 1991 Associated Press news item read, "A year after drivers went on strike, Greyhound Lines is as lean as the purebred canine that's been its symbol for three decades."

❧ *Grayback* ❧

He . . . thinks he's old Grayback from Wayback.

—MARK TWAIN, *A Connecticut Yankee
in King Arthur's Court* (1889)

From the early nineteenth century on, *grayback* has been
a name used loosely for whales and other marine animals
that are dark gray on top and lighter-colored or white on
their underside. This is true of a number of species.

During the American Civil War the name was transferred to mean a Confederate soldier, so called for his
gray uniform. And during this same period, in barracks
and prison camps, *grayback* became a slang term for the
body louse, which tended to become endemic under wartime conditions.

❧ *Old and Gray* ❧

*When you are old and gray and full of sleep,
And nodding by the fire, take down this book.*

—WILLIAM BUTLER YEATS,
When You Are Old (1893)

Gray hair has probably been associated with aging ever
since the first human beings lived long enough for their
hair to turn gray. Occasionally this change occurs sud-
denly as the result of some extremely frightening expe-
rience, or from grief. Byron mentions this eventuality in
The Prisoner of Chillon (1816):

*My hair is grey, but not with years,
Nor grew it white
In a single night,
As men's have grown from sudden fears.*

Actually, it is impossible for one to turn gray in that short a time, unless a person has a lot of gray hair already. Then, however, the remaining dark hairs, if they are in what dermatologists call the resting phase of the hair cycle, may fall out faster than they normally would from the stress of a terrible shock, such as a major operation or the death of a loved one, leaving mainly the gray.

Freed From Gray Hair

Gray hair, like old age, also may be associated with wisdom: "Wisdom is the gray hair unto men, and an unspotted life is old age," holds the writer of the Wisdom of Solomon (4:9) in the Apocrypha.

Similar associations may extend to the *graybeard*, a term used since the sixteenth century as a synonym for an old man. More often, however, this expression is used in a derogatory fashion, implying a man who is doddering with old age. "He is grey before he's good," says a proverb in John Ray's collection of 1678, indicating that a man has reached old age before attaining virtue. Shakespeare, too, disparaged the graybeard: "Graybeard, thy love doth freeze," the young suitor Tranio taunts the old Gremio (*The Taming of the Shrew*, 2:1).

In the eighteenth century the name "graybeard" was also used for a large earthenware jug used to hold spirits. It alluded to the bellarmine, a stoneware container of the sixteenth and seventeenth centuries that was ornamented with a bearded mask (it was named for Cardinal Bellarmino, a sixteenth-century Italian churchman who was the object of this caricature). But this usage, along with the jug, is virtually obsolete.

A far more recent phenomenon is the *Gray Panthers*, an organization founded in the United States in 1970 to combat age discrimination. It took its name from the militantly antiracist BLACK PANTHERS but substituted "gray" in allusion to gray hair and old age. Its members attempted to exert *gray power* (the counterpart of the BLACK POWER movement), lobbying for legislation favorable to the elderly and otherwise undertaking collective action for the benefit of this growing group.

In industrialized nations such as the United States, the increase in life expectancy and the decrease in the birth rate have resulted in a much larger proportion of elderly persons. This phenomenon is often referred to as *graying*, so that we speak of, for example, *the graying of the suburbs*, describing a suburban area whose school enrollment is declining and that has a higher population of retirees.

❧ *Dressed in Gray* ❧

It was a friar of orders gray
Walkt forth to tell his beads.

—THOMAS PERCY,
from *Reliques of
Ancient English Poetry* (1765)

The earliest allusion to gray clothing is the name *Gray Friars*, which has been used for the Franciscan friars since the fourteenth century. For a time other religious orders wearing gray habits, such as the Cistercian monks, also were called "Gray Friars," but the name was used mainly for the order of St. Francis, founded by Francis of Assisi.

Two far more recent allusions to clothing are *banker's gray* and *the man in the gray flannel suit*. The first is a fashion-industry neologism for a shade of medium gray used for conservative men's suits, such as might be worn by bankers. The second was the title of a popular novel (1955) by Sloan Wilson about a New York advertising executive struggling to get ahead and still find meaning in his home life. The gray flannel suit was virtually a uniform for upwardly mobile business executives of this period, and the novel and motion picture based on it (1956) made the term synonymous with that particular life-style.

A decade earlier, some advertising employee not very different from Wilson's protagonist invented the expression *tattletale gray* to persuade consumers to use a particular brand of soap powder and avoid this shameful sign of inadequate laundering. It caught on enough to enter the language permanently (it is, for example, an entry in the 1987 *Random House Unabridged Dictionary*).

Gray water is of more recent provenance, a product of a new emphasis on resource conservation and recycling. It signifies waste water from a sink or washing machine that can be reused for flushing toilets, for example, without risk of contamination. The term dates from the early 1970s, when this practice was suggested as a conservation measure for areas plagued with severe drought, as much of the American West is.

❧ *The Gray Market* ❧

It was pointed out at the beginning of this chapter that gray is an intermediate color, and this sense of it dominates in such expressions as *gray market* and *gray collar*.

The gray market is not a physical marketplace. Rather, it refers to transactions that are conducted outside ordinary business channels but that are not illegal. It exists mainly when there is a huge difference between demand and supply. When demand is high, gray market prices will be high; they reflect the willingness of buyers to pay a premium for scarce goods. When supply is abundant, the gray market will offer sizable discounts. For example, with a product such as a luxury imported sports car, available to American consumers only through authorized dealers, a gray-market entrepreneur might buy the car abroad from the manufacturer, add the antipollution devices mandated by American law, and still be able to undersell the American authorized dealer.

A *gray-collar* job is one midway between BLUE-COLLAR and WHITE-COLLAR employment, or one that contains elements of each. For example, a construction contractor who employs both building trade blue-collar workers (carpenters, electricians, etc.) and their on-the-job supervisors might be considered a gray-collar worker. He does no manual labor himself and performs little direct supervision of blue-collar employees.

The "gray" in gray-collar is not literally made of *gray goods*. This last term is used in the textile industry for woven or knitted fabric as it leaves the loom or knitting machine, before it has been bleached, dyed, or otherwise treated.

🙠 *Gray Eminence* 🙠

Clothing had nothing to do with the invention of *gray eminence*, a translation of a nickname originally used for a Capuchin monk who lived four hundred years ago. The term is a straight translation of the French *éminence grise* and referred to François Le Clerc du Tremblay (1577–1638), also known as Père Joseph. An agent and trusted counselor of Cardinal Richelieu, he devoted himself with equal fervor to missionary work and to the delicate secret diplomatic negotiations he conducted on the Cardinal's behalf. The nickname alluded to his allegedly evil influence over the Cardinal, perhaps likening it to a dark cloud. This view is now thought to have been inaccurate—that is, the Cardinal ruled him, and not vice versa. Nevertheless, the name stuck (Aldous Huxley used it as the title of a book about him in 1941). Later it was extended to mean any secret and powerful influence on a public figure—in effect, the power behind the throne.

🙠 *The Little Gray Cells* 🙠

Since the early nineteenth century the active part of the brain (and of some other nerve tissue) has been called *gray matter*, simply alluding to its color. This term is not much used by present-day physiologists, whose knowledge in this area has become vastly more sophisticated. The term, however, survives, particularly in the form of *little gray cells*, owing to one of the most popular mystery novelists of all time, Agatha Christie. Her insufferably conceited protagonist, the Belgian detective Hercule Poirot, insists that only his superior intelligence will solve the crimes that puzzle the police. A typical example is found in *The Affair at Styles* (1920):

> *He tapped his forehead. "These little grey cells.*
> *It is up to them—as you say over here."*

Fortunately, Poirot was faced mostly with simple murders to solve. He might not have fared so well in sorting out espionage cases involving *graymail*, a neologism of the 1970s. This term came into being through criminal proceedings against accused spies and was used to describe their threats to expose government secrets in a public trial unless the charges against them were dropped. In other words, as Mario Pei explained in his *Double Speak in America* (1973), "I will do something bad to you if you do something bad to me."

Green Pastures

$\mathcal{G}$reen is the color of freshness and renewal, or so it has been in Western culture since earliest times. Reappearing in nature in springtime, after a white or brown winter, it became a symbol of fertility and growth, of abundance and eternal life. "All thing is gay that is greene," was one of John Heywood's *Proverbs* back in 1546, and a sixteenth-century Spanish proverb quoted in James Howell's 1659 collection went even further: "Truth is always green."

Of course, this admiring view is not held in every culture; green is abhorred by some as the color of pus and corruption. But in Europe and the Near East, green has long been venerated. In Islam it is the color borne by the descendants of Muhammad, and hence it appears in nearly every Muslim country's flag.

The word "green" comes from the Old English *gréne*, in turn from *grêne* in old Frisian and various related Germanic languages. On the spectrum it is the color intermediate between blue and yellow. It often is defined as the color of growing grass and leaves, and most similes involving green refer to plants. *Green as grass* and *green as a leek* both date from the fourteenth century, as does *green as emerald*. Heard less often today are *green as young potatoes, green as sap*, and *green as a bottle* (nowadays glass bottles come in all colors).

Although many describe the sea as blue ("the deep blue sea," for example), to some it appears more green, and there is a shade commonly called *sea green*. "Eyes colored like a water flower, and deeper than the sea's green glass," wrote Algernon Charles Swinburne, a poet particularly enamored of color (*Félise*, 1880). And in one of the most famous passages in Shakespeare's *Macbeth*, Macbeth asks if all great Neptune's ocean can cleanse his hands of blood, and says (2:1),

> *No, this my hand will rather*
> *The multitudinous seas incarnadine,*
> *Making the green one red.*

Similarly, hills and mountains are sometimes perceived as green. In fact, a saying recorded in the *Oxford Dictionary of Proverbs* remarks that the hills are green when far away but bare when they are nearby. (Also see GREEN MOUNTAIN BOYS.) That brings to mind a much better-known adage, stated by Erasmus in the sixteenth century and repeated ever since: *The grass is always greener on the other side*—that is, what one doesn't possess or can't attain always looks more appealing than what one has.

Figuratively, although green frequently means "fresh" and "new," it can also mean young, unripe, and immature (see under GREENHORN below). Thus, *green as grass* is sometimes used figuratively, denoting inexperienced and ignorant.

🍂 *Green Pastures* 🍂

Most often, green refers or is likened to grass-covered places. "He maketh me to lie down in green pastures: he leadeth me beside the still waters," from that most familiar of Bible passages, Psalm 23, conjures up the peace of lying in a grassy meadow. From this usage, *green pastures* is sometimes interpreted as paradise, as in Marc Connelly's play *The Green Pastures* (1930), a fantasy of biblical history cast in terms of black southern life.

> *Whose life in low estate began*
> *And on a simple village green.*
>
> —ALFRED, LORD TENNYSON,
> *In Memoriam* (1850)

The green has meant "grass" since the year 1000. From the fifteenth century on, however, the term often was used more specifically to mean *the village green*, a parcel of grassy land that was a relic of the common pasturelands of the medieval manor. It was not owned by any individual but rather was the collective property of all who lived there. Both the practice of reserving a piece of common land and this name were brought to America by the early settlers, and consequently many New England towns still sport a village or town green.

In the seventeenth century a still more specific term came into being, the *bowling green*, a level, grassy plot used for the game of bowls. Also known as lawn bowling or bowling on the green, this game, which is still played, involves rolling one's ball down the length of the green to a point as close as possible to a white ball positioned there. Although the game is no longer as widely popular as it once was, its name has been guaranteed long survival, since it became the place name of a number of localities, among them the towns of Bowling Green in Kentucky and Ohio, and a small open area at the southern end of Manhattan, in New York City.

In the mid-nineteenth century, with the increasing popularity of golf, came a new term, *putting green*, denoting the closely mowed area around each hole. In subsequent years several other golf-related expressions came into use. One was *the rub of the green*, meaning, in effect, the luck of the draw. For example, one golfer's ball might hit a small twig or stone and be so deflected as to roll into the hole, whereas another player's ball, striking the same obstacle, might then miss the hole altogether. The players' skill here would have nothing to do with the outcome; it was the rub of the green. Conceivably one might improve one's chances if one took the time and trouble to *read the green*—that is, analyze the course for the slope and surface of the ground, obstacles, and other relevant characteristics.

?• *Green Grow the Rushes* •?

In long-ago England it was the custom to spread fresh rushes on the floor of a cottage to welcome a guest who had been long absent. Through this practice, *green rushes* became, for a time, an exclamation of surprise and welcome for such a person. Robert Greene wrote of the custom in *Menaphon* (1589), "It is long since we met . . . when you come you shall have green rushes, you are such a stranger."

Though both custom and exclamation have long been obsolete, the term survives in a familiar folk song, *Green Grow the Rushes, Ho!*, one of the few cumulative songs with religious significance. (In such a format, each new

verse is added to the preceding one and repeated all the
way through, as in the Christmas carol *The Twelve Days
of Christmas*.) The precise significance of the "green
rushes" here has been lost.

Among the oldest ballads that is still frequently
heard is *Greensleeves*. First published about 1580, it was
mentioned in the sixteenth century by Shakespeare and
by Beaumont and Fletcher, among others. The music,
particularly the bass—a *passamezzo antico*, an oft-used
Italian pattern—is probably considerably older. The text
tells the tale of a faithless lady, and the refrain is:

> *Greensleeves was my joy,*
> *Greensleeves was my delight,*
> *Greensleeves was my heart of gold,*
> *And who but Lady Greensleeves?*

The "greensleeves" presumably refer to the lady's gown,
but the song became so popular that for a time *greensleeves* became synonymous with an unfaithful woman.

ᔰ *Wearing of the Green* ᔰ

This meaning of "greensleeves" is now obsolete, as is the
contemporary *green gown*. In the sixteenth century, *to
give a green gown* meant to roll in sport with a woman
on the grass, which thus stained her dress. Such sport
also implied, and became synonymous with, loss of her
virginity. Robert Herrick described it in his *Corrina's
Going a-Maying* (1648):

> *And some have wept and woo'd,*
>   *and plighted troth . . .*
> *Many a green-gown has been given,*
> *Many a kiss, both odd and even.*

The green gown in question might perhaps have been of *Lincoln green*, a bright green cloth made in the cathedral town of Lincoln. It became famous for being the garb of Robin Hood and his merry men. It is described in one of the ballads collected by F. J. Child, dating from about 1510: "When they were clothed in Lyncolne grene, they kest away theyre grave." Robin Hood or some forester like him is believed to be the source of the *Green Man*, a very common sign and name for British public houses. (It has no connection with *little green men*, a mid-twentieth-century term for mysterious beings carried to earth by flying saucers; this term, according to Partridge, originated in Canada about 1957 and was further promulgated by horror comics depicting strange little green creatures from outer space.)

The Wearing of the Green, on the other hand, is an Irish patriotic ballad from the late eighteenth century that documents green as the symbolic color of the Irish patriots. "They are hanging men and women for the wearing of the green," it went. Blessed with ample rainfall and a mild climate, Ireland is famous for its bright-green vegetation. William Drennan, an eighteenth-century poet, dubbed it *the Emerald Isle* in his poem *Erin*, a name that stuck, along with *Green Erin*. Not unnaturally, green became the color of the Nationalist Party and has remained symbolic of Ireland ever since.

🙠 *Greenhorn* 🙠

You speak like a green girl.

—WILLIAM SHAKESPEARE,
Hamlet, 1:3

Green has been used figuratively to describe unripe and immature *things* since about 1300 and *individuals* since

the mid-sixteenth century. "Unlearned and raw or grene
in cunning," wrote Nicholas Udall in his 1548 translation
of Erasmus's biblical commentaries. By the seventeenth
century we also had the expression *greenhorn*, denoting
a rank beginner or novice. It no doubt alludes to the soft
"green" horns of a young deer or steer. Another similar
expression was *green hand*, for an inexperienced sailor.

❧ *Under the Greenwood Tree* ❧

Eating *green apples* might well cause one to *turn green*
with indigestion, unless the apples were *greenings*. As
pointed out, green has long meant unripe, but in the
seventeenth century the name "greening" was given to

a variety of pear, and later a kind of apple, that was ripe even though its skin remained green in color. The same was true of the *greengage plum*, a variety introduced to Britain from France by Sir William Gage about 1725 and named in his honor.

As seen above, a green hand signified inexperience. Not so *green fingers* or a *green thumb*, both of which denote a considerable aptitude for making things grow. They are particularly useful in the *greenhouse*, a name used since the seventeenth century for a glass enclosure in which tender plants and/or plants out of season are nurtured. "Who loves a garden loves a greenhouse too," wrote poet William Cowper (*The Garden*, 1785).

In contrast to the contents of greenhouses, *greens*, a staple of the American southern kitchen, are not particularly delicate. This name is used loosely for a large variety of leafy green vegetables, such as beet tops, collards, turnip leaves, mustard and dandelion greens, kale, Swiss chard, chicory, romaine, and various kinds of lettuce. In the South they are often cooked in bacon or pork fat. Nowadays greens can be bought at a supermarket, but in earlier times, if they did not come from one's own garden, they might be purchased from a *greengrocer*. This expression has been used for a retailer specializing in vegetables and fruits since the early eighteenth century. It may have been invented by one such storekeeper who advertised his wares in the *London Gazette* in 1723. And it was still current in the late nineteenth century, when W. S. Gilbert wrote the lyrics of the Lord Chancellor's nightmare song in *Iolanthe* (1882), "From the greengrocer tree you get grapes and green pea . . ."

> *Under the greenwood tree,*
> *Who loves to lie with me.*
>
> —WILLIAM SHAKESPEARE,
> *As You Like It*, 5:1

In a roundabout way that gets us to *greenwood*, which since the fourteenth century has meant a wood or forest in full leaf. From the sixteenth century on it acquired another connotation, that of the typical surroundings of outlaw life, such as pursued by the likes of Robin Hood. This is what is meant in the ballad *The Nut Brown Maid*, "For I must to the greenwood go, alone, a banished man."

The two-word version of *green wood* has another meaning as well, that of unseasoned, uncured wood. While such wood might be expected to yield a good deal of smoke when burned, a fifteenth-century proverb maintains that "The grene wode is hotter than the other whan it is wel kyndeled." On the other hand, Walter de la Mare said, "Of all the trees in England . . . Only the Ash, the bonnie Ash burns fierce while it is green" (*Trees*, 1920).

An analogy to green wood is the source of the term *greenstick fracture*, found in medical texts since about 1885. It describes the fracture of a long bone where one side is broken and the other side merely bent. This kind of trauma occurs mainly in children, whose bones are still soft, so that they bend rather than snap.

🎄 *The Green Revolution* 🎄

Greenery, a word that signifies foliage or vegetation in general and that was probably invented by Samuel Taylor Coleridge, is dear to the hearts of a late twentieth-century political movement. "Here were forests ancient as the hills, Enfolding sunny spots of greenery," rhapsodized Coleridge (*Kubla Khan*, 1797). But in the course of the next two centuries, what was happening to these serendipitous spaces? Gradually they were being replaced by housing, factories, roads, parking lots—all the phenomena of Western progress.

Although since the early 1930s some British and

American localities have established zoning laws to maintain a *green belt*, as officially designated open lands are called, conservationists have protested that there are far too few of these to make a difference. Moreover, burgeoning industry and concomitant pollution raised a new threat, *the greenhouse effect*, a term first surfacing in a meteorological textbook of 1937. Owing to various emissions, the surface and lower atmosphere of our planet have been experiencing higher and higher temperatures because of the greater transparency of the atmosphere to visible solar radiation. The earth has been growing warmer and carbon dioxide levels have been increasing, both sources of grave concern to scientists.

Conservationists and environmentalists had been muttering about these matters for some time, but in the early 1970s they began to organize a strong environmentalist lobby, at first in West Germany and later in other countries as well. They were called the *Green Party*, derived from the German *Grüne Aktion Zukunft* (Green Campaign for the Future) and originating as an outgrowth of anti-nuclear-power campaigns. They made lists of political candidates who supported their views (so-called *green lists*) and eventually fielded their own candidates for office. Loosely known as *the Greens*, they tried to increase their influence, which came to be called *green power* (analogous to BLACK POWER and GRAY POWER).

A related organization was founded in Canada in 1971. Called *Greenpeace* and dedicated to nonviolent measures, it supported a variety of conservation causes and obtained considerable publicity in its campaigns to protect whales and young seals as well as to ban all nuclear testing.

One might think that the *Green Revolution* would describe the success of these groups, but although this term dates from approximately the same time, it refers to a quite different project. In the 1960s extremely high-yield hybrids of cereal crops, mainly wheat, rice, and corn,

were developed specifically for the overpopulated, un-
derfed nations of Asia. Through use of such seed, it was
hoped, food production would increase rapidly. However,
the new hybrid strains proved to be a mixed blessing.
They required better cultivation, especially more water
and more fertilizer, than the older types, and consequently more irrigation equipment as well as other machinery and pesticides were needed, offsetting some of
their economic benefits.

🙚 *Green Cheese* 🙚

> *You may as soon persuade some Country Peasant
> that the Moon is made of Green Cheese (as we
> say) as that 'tis bigger than his Cart-Wheel.*
>
> —JOHN WILKINS,
> *Discourse Concerning A New World* (1638)

So-called *green cheese* had been manufactured for years
—it was first mentioned in *Piers Ploughman* (1362)—and
could mean any of three kinds: new fresh cheese; inferior
cheese, made from skim milk or whey; or cheese colored
with sage or some other green herb. Some writers speculate that associating the moon with green cheese is derived from the last kind, the moon's variegated surface
vaguely resembling a cheese mixed with sage. Even without sophisticated astronomical knowledge, it would be
hard to believe the moon was actually so constituted.
Hence, by the early sixteenth century, to make someone
believe that the moon is made of green cheese meant to
convince someone of a total absurdity.

Presumably only the most gullible could be conned
in this way. One way of characterizing such a person was
to see green in his/her eye, meaning to detect gullibility.
This turn of phrase dates from the mid-nineteenth cen-

tury but is not often heard today. James Barrie still had it in his play *Sentimental Tommy* (1896): "Do you see any green in my eye, my dear?"

❧ *Green Sickness* ❧

Jaundice, a symptom of liver disease, makes the whites of the patient's eyes look yellow, not green. Nevertheless, in the nineteenth century a serious variety of jaundice, from which patients rarely recovered, was called the *green sickness*. Back in the sixteenth century this same name had been used for a mild form of anemia that today is generally known as chlorosis; it occurs mainly in adolescent girls and gives their skin a yellow-greenish cast.

We sometimes describe someone who looks ill, especially with nausea or a similar stomach upset, as looking *green about the gills*. "A plate of turtle green and glutinous," as described by Robert Browning (*The Pied Piper of Hamelin*, 1842), might make that happen to those who don't find *green turtle* a delicacy. However, we also characterize a quite different sickness as "green"—the disease of pathological jealousy. The source probably lies in the old association of a greenish, bilious complexion not only with illness but also with ill humor, fear, and jealousy. "She pined in thought, with a green and yellow melancholy," wrote Shakespeare in *Twelfth Night* (2:4). And in *Antony and Cleopatra* (3:2) Enobarbus reports that Lepidus "is troubled with the green sickness."

But far better known is the Bard's *green-eyed monster*. It comes from *Othello* (3:3), where the villain Iago tells Othello, "O! beware, my lord, of jealousy; it is the green-ey'd monster which doth mock the meat it feeds on." The poet here is alluding to the green-eyed cat family, who are known for teasing their prey, seeming to love and hate them at the same time, but elsewhere he directly associated green-eyed with jealous, specifically in *The*

Merchant of Venice, where Portia speaks of "green-eyed jealousy" (3:2).

The green-eyed monster caught on almost immediately and today remains synonymous with jealousy. John Milton and Percy Bysshe Shelley are among the great poets who adopted it. "Jealousy's eyes are green," wrote Shelley (*Swellfoot the Tyrant*). Today we also are apt to describe someone as being *green with envy*, which is almost but not quite the same emotion as jealousy. One might say that whereas Othello fell prey to the green-eyed monster, Iago plotted his master's downfall because he was green with envy of Othello's great success and popularity.

❧ *Red Light, Green Light* ❧

April prepares her green traffic light and the world thinks Go.

—CHRISTOPHER MORLEY, *John Mistletoe* (1932)

An old children's game popular at birthday parties involves one child directing the others to move or stand still by calling out "Green light" or "Red light."

By the early 1880s, when railroads had become an important means of transportation, standard signals had come into use on the tracks, a red light signifying "stop" and a green one "go." This practice, of course, is used to the present day, not only for trains but also for automobiles and other kinds of traffic. Moreover, by the 1930s these terms had begun to be used figuratively, so that *to give the green light* to something or someone meant to give permission to proceed. Playwright Terrence Rattigan used it in *French Without Tears* (1937): "We had a bottle of wine and got pretty gay, and all the time she was giving me the old green light" (3:1).

Just as well that it was wine, and not the *green peril*, as the French liqueur absinthe was called from the 1880s on. Bright green in color and consisting of 70 to 80 percent alcohol (140 to 160 proof in modern-day terms), it was considered a virtually lethal potion. Excessive consumption affected not only the liver and other digestive organs but the nervous system as well, producing delirium and idiocy. In the early decades of the twentieth century its manufacture was outlawed in Switzerland and France, the main sources of supply.

🙣 *Green Stuff* 🙣

It is hard to imagine an era when money consisted principally of gold and silver and copper, but that was the case in 1862, when the U.S. Treasury issued the first *greenbacks*. Plagued by a shortage of gold and silver to finance the Civil War, the Treasury issued a total of $450 million in notes backed solely by the credit of the United States and which were simply declared to be legal tender. It was Secretary of the Treasury Salmon P. Chase who is thought to have been the first to call the notes "greenbacks," because green ink was used to print the back sides.

The question of redeeming these greenbacks remained a burning political issue for the next two decades. Their name was adopted by a political party, the *Greenback Labor Party*, which showed considerable strength in the congressional elections of 1878. In that year Congress decided that the nearly $347 million outstanding in greenbacks should remain a permanent part of the nation's money supply, and by the end of the year the notes for the first time attained a face value in gold.

The widespread use of paper money no doubt encouraged individuals with printing skills and equipment to produce some of their own. In the late nineteenth century the term *green goods* began to be widely used for counterfeit dollars. In fact, the *Congressional Record* of January 29, 1889, documents the term as a euphemism: "There are various terms used to avoid the use of the ugly words 'counterfeit money,' the most common one being 'green goods' " (according to Representative B. A. Enloe of Tennessee). Although Eric Partridge held that the term became standard American English, it is no longer heard much and may be obsolete. Not so for *green stuff*, an American slang expression current since about 1950 for money.

A newer nefarious but perfectly legal practice is *greenmail*, a corporate version of BLACKMAIL. Greenmail involves buying a large block of a company's stock and then threatening to take over the company, with the expectation that to thwart a takeover those shares will be bought back at a significant premium over the market price. Although the practice no doubt existed earlier, this name for it first appeared in print in the early 1980s.

Another monetary neologism that may or may not survive is *greentapping*, a method of automatically making donations to some worthy cause in the course of an ordinary commercial transaction. For example, the holder of a bank credit card might assign 1 percent of the money owed on her bill to organizations working to eliminate world hunger. At this writing, the mechanism for such donations is not widespread, and both the practice and this name for it may turn out to be short-lived.

❧ *From Greenland's Icy Mountains* ❧

The title of this hymn by Bishop Reginald Heber (1783–1826) echoes the general sentiment about this northern outpost, which lies largely within the Arctic Circle. Its name, however, was a calculated deception. It was chosen by Eric the Red about the year 986 or so in order to attract settlers to its shores. It is hard to say how many were fooled, and for how long. In the nineteenth century *cold as Greenland* was a common simile in America, dispelling any surviving illusions about its climate.

More accurate nomenclature was used for the *Green Mountain Boys*, "so called from their residing within the limits of the Green Mountain," according to W. Gordon's *History of the American Revolution.* They came, of course, from Vermont, whose name is from the French for "green mountain," *vert mont.* The Green Mountain Boys were originally organized by Ethan Allen to fight out a land dispute with New York and New Hampshire. When the colonies rebelled against Britain, the Green Mountain Boys joined the fight and, although only a tiny force, surprised and captured the British garrison at Fort Ticonderoga in New York. In 1777 Vermont was declared an independent state and adopted the nickname *Green Mountain State.* Unlike Greenland's, its name is not a misnomer. The Green Mountains' highest peak is Mount Mansfield, 4,393 feet high and wooded right to the top. So except when covered by snow, the mountains are indeed green.

❧ *The Green Room* ❧

The *green room*, where performers rest between acts and receive admirers, has been so called since the late seventeenth century. Playwright Colly Cibber mentioned it in his 1701 play *Love Makes the Man.* Presumably the term came from a tradition of painting the walls of these rooms green, perhaps, as some suggest, because this color is restful to the eyes, which have been exposed to bright footlights. Today's green rooms can be painted any color, but the term survives.

Tired performers may find themselves plagued by too many well-wishers, although that is not very likely. Ball players, on the other hand, may be plagued by *greenflies*. In the seventeenth century a greenfly was simply an artificial fly used by fishermen in search of the elusive trout. In the eighteenth century the name was attached to the pesky green aphid, which attacks fruit trees. But beginning in the late 1970s the name was used for a kind of devoted baseball fan who goes to extraordinary lengths to meet major-league players, obtain their autographs, appear with them in photographs, and the like. It is too early to say if this American slang usage will be as persistent as the type of person so designated.

🐌 *Green Berets and Green Cards* 🐌

Two other terms gained prominence in the second half of the twentieth century. The *Green Berets* first was a nickname for the British Commandos, highly trained special forces whose uniform included a green beret. In the 1950s the name began to be used for the U.S. Special Forces, Army personnel especially trained to instruct and assist indigenous forces in guerrilla warfare and counterrevolutionary activities. The Green Berets became widely known for their role in the Vietnam War, where, depending on one's view of this controversial conflict, they were heroes or villains (or perhaps both).

The *green card* is also a British term that crossed the Atlantic, but with an entirely different meaning. In Britain, beginning in the 1950s, motorists were required to carry a green card as evidence that they had third-party insurance. In the United States, beginning in the 1960s, individuals who lacked American citizenship were required to obtain an official card, originally green in color, which gave them permission to work in the United States. Basically the issuance of green cards was an attempt to curtail illegal immigration, but it met with mixed success, even when new laws imposed penalties on employers for hiring anyone who lacked one.

Agent Orange

*O*range is the only color of the spectrum that was named for an object. The fruit called orange originated in Southeast Asia and came to Europe during the Saracen conquest and the Crusades. The fruit comes from an evergreen tree, *Citrus aurantium*, and the word "orange," from the Old French *orenge*, has been used in English since about 1300. The color is, of course, the reddish-yellow of the fruit; on the spectrum it lies between red and yellow.

In folklore the color orange stands for fire and flames, health, lust, vigor, and wholesomeness. In heraldry the color is called *tenne* or *tawney*. Because the tree is evergreen and everbearing, it became associated with fruitfulness. The Roman god Jupiter gave Juno an orange at their wedding, and some believe this is the origin of the ORANGE BLOSSOM (see below) as a bridal flower.

The Orange, that is too hard squeez'd, yields a bitter Juice.

—THOMAS FULLER, *Gnomologia* (1732)

Oranges have long been prized as a particularly juicy fruit. *Orangeade*, a drink made of orange juice diluted with water and sweetened with sugar, dates from the sixteenth century, and just plain orange juice had probably been drunk for much longer. By the seventeenth century, *to squeeze* or *suck an orange* was being used figuratively to mean taking all the profit out of something or someone, which/who was then discarded. "So soon as the Orange is squeezed, it's thrown upon the ground," wrote Baltasar Gracian (*The Courtier's Outlook*, 1685). In 1751 the French philosopher Voltaire used this metaphor for his own treatment at the hands of Frederick the Great, with whom he had quarreled: "They squeeze the orange, throw away the skin," he wrote in a letter to a friend (in French; but it reads the same in translation).

🙠 *Orange Blossoms* 🙠

The orange flower perfumes the bower.

—SIR WALTER SCOTT,
The Monastery (1820)

The flower of the orange tree, the orange blossom, became symbolic of the marriage ceremony in Britain about 1820, when the custom of using it for wedding decorations was imported from France. It combined two symbols. The white flower stood for purity, innocence, and chastity; and the orange, a remarkably prolific tree, stood for fertility. Folklore decreed that as a nuptial flower the orange blossom must be discarded before it withers, or it will bring on barrenness. Although this notion itself seems to have been discarded, orange blossoms are still a traditional wedding flower, used in the bride's wreath, bouquets, and other decorations.

In the 1920s the flower's name was adopted for a cocktail. Considered a drink suitable for ladies, this *orange blossom* consisted of the juice of half an orange and an equal amount of gin, shaken with cracked ice and strained.

Since the state of Florida is a major producer of oranges, it seems logical that it adopted the orange blossom as its state flower. It also was the first state to imitate California's Rose Bowl, an important feature of college football since 1902, and in 1935 set up the *Orange Bowl*, still eagerly followed by fans.

According to Eric Partridge's compendium of underworld slang, *orange bowl* also had a more sinister meaning, beginning about 1925: it denoted a large, half-orange shell used as a shade for an opium lamp.

In Florida and California oranges are grown outdoors. In colder climates the trees could not survive, which was the reason for building an *orangery*, a kind of greenhouse specifically used to cultivate orange trees. Both the custom and the name came to England from France in the seventeenth century. Among the most famous such enclosures is Paris's *L'Orangerie* (as the French spell it), a pavilion in the Tuileries Gardens that was built in the first half of the nineteenth century, during the Second Empire. A charming structure in a delightful setting, it has served as an art gallery since the beginning of the twentieth century.

Civil as an orange, and something of that jealous complexion.

—WILLIAM SHAKESPEARE,
Much Ado About Nothing, 2:1

Shakespeare was not the only poet to describe the color orange in a confusing fashion. The above-quoted citation appears to mix it up with either yellow or green, both colors identified with jealousy. A few decades later Andrew Marvell had it closer to gold, in his *Bermudas* (1681):

He hangs in shades the orange bright,
Like golden lamps in a green night.

Tennyson was somewhat closer to the mark in his description of a sunset (*Mariana in the South,* 1832):

Till all the crimson changed, and past
Into deep orange o'er the sea.

And then we have *orange pekoe tea,* which is not orange at all. A type of black tea, it is first mentioned in Cassell's 1879 dictionary of cookery. At one stage in its journey from bush to tea bag it is indeed orange, but that still is not the source of the name.

In processing, the tea leaves are spread on trays to "wither"—to lose their crispness and become limp. They are then passed under large rollers that break them up and release the essential oils that cause fermentation or oxidation. They are again spread out and, absorbing oxygen from the air, they oxidize, gradually losing their green color and turning a bright, coppery (dark-orange) shade. However, the next step, drying the leaves, changes them to their familiar black color. When the tea is dried it is ready to be sorted into grades and packed for shipment. Defying logic, it is at this point that the term "orange pekoe" is used to indicate a particular leaf size, obtained by sifting.

The *orange stick* isn't orange either, and never was. This little manicure aid, used since about 1900 to push back cuticle, is simply a slender, rounded stick with tapered ends. It originally was made from the wood of the orange tree, which is hard, fine-grained, and light yellowish in color. Today orange sticks are not necessarily made from this material, but the name has persisted nevertheless.

🐾 *William of Orange* 🐾

England's King William III was also called William of Orange, after the territory along France's Rhône River that was acquired by his ancestors (largely through marriage rather than conquest). Originally it consisted just of the ancient town of Arausio, north of Avignon. Arausio later was renamed Orange and greatly enlarged. William himself secured his future by marrying Princess Mary, the Protestant daughter of James of York, who was to become King James II. A dozen years later English Protestant nobles, who were increasingly dissatisfied with the Roman Catholic James II, invited William and his bride to take the English throne. He did, in what has ever since been called the Glorious Revolution of 1689, accomplished without any bloodshed whatever. However, the following year he did have to engage James II and his Catholic supporters at the Battle of the Boyne, where James was defeated and then fled to France.

The coincidence of William's name with that of the color for a time created a new fashion: His supporters wore orange-colored ribbons, scarves, and cockades to signify their allegiance. The House of Orange still reigns in the Netherlands, where William himself was born, but today its associations with the color are purely coincidental.

☙ *Orangemen* ☙

More than a century later, in 1795, the Loyal Orange Institution was founded in the Irish province of Ulster. Dedicated to defending Protestantism in Ireland, it chose its name in commemoration of the Protestant victory at the Boyne under William of Orange, and its members were called *Orangemen.* Today the anniversary of this battle, July 12, and the date of William's first landing in England, November 5, are celebrated by the society as important holidays, on which the members wear orange flowers and orange-colored sashes and march in parades.

☙ *Orange Free State* ☙

The *Orange Free State*, today one of the Republic of South Africa's four provinces, was originally founded about 1824 by Dutch settlers who trekked north after Great Britain seized the Cape of Good Hope in 1806. The Orange Free State was named for the Dutch House of Orange, as was the great Orange River, which runs along its boundary. Annexed by the British in 1848, it became a republic six years later, and a British colony after the British won the Boer War (1902). It became self-governing in 1907 and joined the Union of South Africa in 1910. Since the mid-nineteenth century the Orange Free State has been known for its valuable gold and diamond mines.

🐝 *Agent Orange* 🐝

In the late 1960s U.S. Air Force fliers dumped millions of gallons of an oily, powerful herbicide and defoliant called *Agent Orange* over the thick jungles of war-ravaged South Vietnam. Rained down on more than five million acres, this chemical was intended to strip the land of crops and of concealing jungle.

Apart from devastating much of the land, the use of Agent Orange gave rise to a bitter controversy among scientists and policymakers. The herbicide contains dioxide, a deadly chemical that causes cancer in laboratory animals. More than 35,000 American veterans of Vietnam have pressed the U.S. government to compensate them for injuries and illnesses they believe were caused by exposure to Agent Orange.

Although there is no doubt that Agent Orange causes cancer and birth defects in animals, it has not been conclusively proved that it has the same effect in human beings. Moreover, with the passage of time the blood of veterans who were exposed to dioxin no longer reveals its presence, or how much ever was present, hampering epidemiological studies. In 1990 the Centers for Disease Control finally released the results of a five-year study that showed that Vietnam veterans are more likely than the rest of the population to get a rare, fatal cancer called non-Hodgkin's lymphoma. Even so, this cancer is extremely rare, striking about 1.5 in 10,000. Still, the government decided to compensate those veterans who had contracted this cancer, which still left some 33,000 veterans with unsatisfied claims. Results of another study published in 1991 indicate that exposure to Agent Orange may have caused a higher incidence of diabetes. Before all the results are in, still other disorders may be implicated.

Actually, four herbicidal spraying materials were used in these attacks: Agent Blue, Agent Purple, Agent

White, and Agent Orange. They were so called from the color of the code stripe on each of their containers. But Agent Orange was the most toxic, and therefore the most memorable of them.

🥭 *A Clockwork Orange* 🥭

> *Who ever heard of a clockwork orange? . . . The attempt to impose upon man . . . laws and conditions appropriate to a mechanical creation, against this I raise my sword-pen.*
>
> —ANTHONY BURGESS,
> *A Clockwork Orange* (1962)

The English writer's novel of this title concerns the transformation of a violent, severely disturbed man by exposing him to an extreme form of aversion therapy—that is, conditioning him to detest the kinds of behavior he had formerly enjoyed. Burgess took his title from a cockney expression applied to homosexuals in Britain from the 1950s, *queer as a clockwork orange*. Although picturesque, calling up the picture of an organism (an orange) into which machinery had been inserted, this turn of phrase probably would never have crossed the Atlantic and gained currency were it not for the fact that this strange and moving novel was made into a motion picture by Stanley Kubrick in 1971. The film, which graphically treated the story as a scathing satire on society in the not too distant future, aroused a good deal of controversy. It was considered offensive by many, and a work of genius by many others. As a result, *clockwork orange* entered the language, meaning a person deprived of individuality by scientific conditioning, which turned him or her into an automaton. It remains to be seen whether or not the expression will survive.

Tickled Pink
with a
Rosy Future

*T*he name "pink" for the color pink began to be used only in the eighteenth century. Prior to that time a *pink* was any of numerous species of the flower genus *Dianthus*, such as carnations, many (but not all) of which are pink in color.

There are at least two theories about the origin of the flower's name. One holds that it alludes to the edges of the blossom's petals, which are notched, or *pinked*. (The verb "to pink" means to pierce, notch, or perforate, and survives in the modern sewing aid *pinking shears*). The other theory, subscribed to by John Ciardi, among others, is that it comes from the Middle Dutch *pinck* or *pincke*, meaning "small," and particularly from *pincke oogen*, or "small eyes," and alludes to the appearance of some of these flowers, especially the moss pink (also called "creeping phlox").

Whichever the case, the color pink is a kind of light red, ranging from pale to quite deep. In folklore pink is a symbol of joy and youth, as well as being associated with the birth of a girl baby, a tradition commercially exploited by manufacturers and sellers of baby products.

❧ *The Flower of Perfection* ❧

In the sixteenth century a pink was considered a delightful flower, as it still is by many gardeners, and so its name began to be used figuratively as "the flower of perfection," the embodiment of the very best possible. Shakespeare was one of the first to use it in this sense: "I am the very pink of courtesy" (*Romeo and Juliet*, 2:4). Jonathan Swift recorded the same usage in his *Polite Conversation* (1738), and Oliver Goldsmith was even more fulsome, with "the very pink of perfection" (*She Stoops to Conquer*, 1:1, 1773), and again, "the very pink of courtesy and circumspection" (same play, Act 4). Even Robert Burns used it, in *The Posie*:

> And I will pu' the pink, the emblem
>   o' my dear,
> For she's the pink o' womankind, and
>   blooms without a peer.

The expression survives today in somewhat different form: We say we're *in the pink* when we mean excellent health, the best possible physical condition. This usage has been around for a while. The *OED* says it has meant "in perfect condition" from the eighteenth century and, more specifically, "in perfect health" from the early 1900s.

❧ *Tickled Pink* ❧

The connotation of excellent health, if not the precise wording, also appeared earlier, as in

> *My face is pink, my hair is sleek,*
> *I dine at Blenheim once a week.*

This ditty was included in the *Masque of Balliol*, composed at this Oxford college in the late 1870s by assorted gentlemen and scholars; it conjures up the image of a neat, prosperous, well-fed individual.

One may also, of course, turn *pink in the face* with physical effort, anger, suppressed laughter, and numerous other emotions that cause a rush of blood to the face. Possibly this was the source of *Strike me pink!*, an expression of indignation or astonishment used in the early 1900s much as one might say, "I'll be damned!"

A more graphic image is to be *tickled pink*, which presumably refers to one's face turning red with laughter when one is tickled. In contravention of those child psychologists who consider tickling, like other kinds of teasing, a form of concealed hostility, this expression has always meant to be overcome with pleasure or amusement. In short, *I am tickled pink* means "I am delighted." The expression first appeared in print in 1922 and continues to be current.

Finally, Eric Partridge cites still another meaning for *to turn pink*: to turn state's evidence. This expression, he believed, came from the criminal slang expression "pink" as an abbreviation first for Pinkerton detective and then for any kind of law-and-order figure, including the ordinary policeman.

❧ *Pink Politics* ❧

*He's nuts on this red-hunting business, and the
pinks are worse than the reds, he says.*

—Upton Sinclair, *Oil!* (1927)

The color *red* has been a symbol for anarchy and revolution since the eighteenth century, and perhaps even
longer. By the early nineteenth century, *pink*, which
might be regarded as a watered-down form of red, was
being used to symbolize political radicalism.

In the twentieth century, after Russian Communists
had adopted a red flag as the international symbol of
socialism and themselves began to be called *Reds*, the
terms *pink*, *pinko*, and *parlor pink* all began to be used
for Communist or leftist sympathizers. They were applied
mainly to those who strongly approved of the changes
wrought by the Communist Revolution in the Soviet
Union but who stopped short of joining the Communist
Party.

These expressions were nearly always used pejora-
tively. In the 1920s and 1930s they were applied principally by anti-Communists to supporters of communism.
However, by the 1940s they also were being used more
generally to disparage anyone perceived to have leftist
or even merely more liberal views than the finger-pointer
himself, a usage that continues to the present day.

Such name-calling took on sinister implications during the 1950s in the hearings held by Senator Joseph
McCarthy, who believed that the United States was rid-
dled with Communist infiltrators and who carried on a
veritable witch-hunt aimed at rooting them out. During
this period even a hint that someone might be "pink"
could have dire consequences.

❧ *Pink Pursuits* ❧

The feminist movement of the 1970s gave us *pink collar* to describe the occupations in which women workers predominate—clerical work, teaching, and retail sales. They were singled out for attack by feminists because they tend to be low-paying, routine, and dead-end positions, without prospects for advancement in salary, responsibility, or status.

"Working women are still disproportionately herded into so-called pink-collar jobs," *Time* magazine proclaimed in 1977. The "pink" in this expression, which is a counterpart of BLUE COLLAR, GRAY COLLAR, and WHITE COLLAR, does not refer to any uniform or clothing. Rather, it alludes to the traditional association of pink with female.

In contrast, the expressions *pink coat* and *hunting pinks* do refer to colored garb but in a rather odd way. The traditional clothing worn in the aristocratic sport of fox hunting includes a scarlet coat, which has been described as "pink" in Great Britain since the 1830s and in America since about 1850. Thus Thomas Hughes wrote, in *Tom Brown at Oxford* (1861), "They are the hunting set, and come in with pea-coats over their pinks." The source of this seeming color blindness is hard to explain. Perhaps hunting in bad weather makes the scarlet fade to pink. In any case, it is a rather broad interpretation of the color designation.

❧ With Pinkie Crooked ❧

The little finger of each hand has been called a *pinkie* (or *pinky*) since the sixteenth century or so. John Ciardi believes this use of pink also comes from the Dutch *pinck* for small, and here most etymologists are inclined to agree. Crooking the little finger so that it sticks out as one grasps a glass or teacup handle was long considered more genteel than holding it with all five fingers, and well-mannered ladies and gentlemen in hunting pinks would certainly have done so. Today the crooked pinkie is apt to be considered a silly affectation.

A now obsolete Americanism of the late nineteenth century is the term *pink tea* for a formal tea party or reception. The source of this expression has been lost, but it may have come from the temperance movement. An 1886 article in the *Weekly Manitoba Liberal* reports on a WCTU Tea where the ladies in charge wore pink caps and aprons and some of the men patrons wore pink ties. The term was also used by Theodore Roosevelt in a letter he wrote in 1905 concerning diplomats who were more interested in form than substance: "There are a large number of well-meaning ambassadors . . . who belong to what I call the pink-tea type." Although contemporary mores would require a high degree of social skill on such occasions, Roosevelt hardly intended his comment as a compliment.

🐦 *Pink Drinks* 🐦

There is no actual beverage called "pink tea," but *pink champagne* has been so described since the early nineteenth century. It actually is either a champagne made from rosé wine or a mixture of champagne and red wine. J. Kenyon rhapsodized about it in 1838: "Lily on liquid roses floating—So floats yon foam o'er pink champagne."

Prohibition saw the invention of numerous exotic cocktails, at least some of which were devised to mask the otherwise raw taste of homemade liquor. One was *pink gin*, a mixture of gin and grenadine; the latter ingredient gave the drink a pink color. Somewhat later, in the 1940s, a bartender invented the *pink lady*, a basic mixture of gin, grenadine, and egg white, to which lemon juice, cream, or still another ingredient might be added. The grenadine again lent it a pink color, and when the mixture was shaken the egg white made it frothy, supposedly like "ladies." (The name "pink lady" later also was used for volunteer hospital aides who wore a pink apron or uniform, similar to those called "candy stripers" for the red-and-white-striped uniform they wore. In the late 1960s it acquired still another meaning, a barbiturate.)

For a time it appeared to be fashionable to *paint the town pink*, a saying both preceded and survived by PAINT THE TOWN RED and carrying the same meaning—to go on a lively and usually drunken spree. James Joyce used the expression in *Ulysses* (1922): "He was at the end of his tether after having often painted town tolerably pink."

Overindulgence of this kind might lead one to see *pink elephants*, which obviously don't inhabit any zoo. This term for visual hallucinations experienced after heavy drinking has been used in America since about 1900 (and came to Britain somewhat later; the *OED*'s earliest citation dates from 1940).

ᵃ *Pink Maladies* ᵃ

> *Come, thou monarch of the vine,*
> *Plumpy Bacchus with pink eyne.*
>
> —WILLIAM SHAKESPEARE,
> *Antony and Cleopatra,* 2:7

Today the first thing conjured up by *pinkeye* is its medical synonym, conjunctivitis. In the sixteenth century, however, it simply meant to have narrow or half-closed eyes; the Greek god of wine and merriment, Bacchus, is often pictured in this way. This kind of pinkeye probably came from the Middle Dutch *pinck*, for small, and had nothing to do with the color.

In the late eighteenth century, however, pinkeye was being used, as a noun, for a kind of potato with pink "eyes," or buds. The modern meaning, for acute inflammation of the conjunctiva, which makes the eyelids and eyes look irritated and pink, dates only from the nineteenth century.

In the late nineteenth century, when widespread advertising for various patent medicines came to the forefront, an extremely well-known ad for a tonic was "Dr. Williams' *pink pills for pale people.*" Although this popular remedy and its familiar slogan were obsolete by the mid-twentieth century, it was still included in the 1986 edition of Eric Partridge's compendium of catchphrases, allegedly because it was still well remembered.

In the modern pharmaceutical industry, new medications being tested are often compared in efficacy to a *little pink pill.* In controlled experiments, one group of patients is given the drug being tested and another group a placebo, a substance having no pharmacological effect. It is the placebo that has been nicknamed "little pink pill," although in proper blind testing it looks exactly like the real drug, and no one—neither patient nor doctor— knows who is receiving a medication and who gets a placebo. The same little pink pill, often consisting of sugar or some harmless substance, may be given by physicians to certain patients, who are told it is a medicine to relieve their symptoms. Often it actually does so, even when the symptoms are real rather than imagined—an example of the mind-body effect whose mysteries have not yet been plumbed.

Still another term from the advertising world is *pink toothbrush*, a threat made in the 1930s by the makers of Ipana toothpaste to scare consumers into using their product. Only regular use of Ipana, they proclaimed on radio and in print ads, would prevent bleeding gums, revealed by the dreaded pink toothbrush.

Much as one might sneer at the claims of modern advertising, present-day dentists do insist that proper dental hygiene will prevent gum disease, the cause of bleeding gums and, if uncontrolled, the loss of one's teeth. It is not, of course, any particular toothpaste that prevents this malady, but never mind: The Ipana people weren't entirely wrong.

❧ The Dreaded Pink Slip ❧

A pink trip slip for a five-cent fare.

—ANONYMOUS,
late nineteenth century

In the days of horse-drawn streetcars, one might actually have received a pink slip of paper representing a fare receipt. The line above comes from an oft-quoted poem about such transport and has been attributed to numerous writers, including Mark Twain.

In the first half of the twentieth century, a *pink slip* most often referred to an article of lingerie, especially in the United States. It was (and is) a woman's sleeveless undergarment, with shoulder straps, and extends from above the bust to the hemline of her skirt or dress. Made of silk, rayon, or cotton, it frequently was pink in color.

Today, however, ladies' slips come in all colors of the rainbow, and the term *pink slip* most often denotes a notice of dismissal from one's employment. This usage dates from about 1910 and presumably originated because at one time it was customary to use pink paper for such notices. However, the expression became much more common about the mid-twentieth century, when it also began to appear in verb form, that is, *to pink-slip* someone meant to fire him or her. Today, even though dismissal notices might appear on white or any other color of paper, the expression "pink slip" remains firmly attached to them.

ஒ *The Rosy Future* ஒ

The words *rose* and *rosy* for a pinkish red, the typical color of wild-growing rose shrubs, is much older than the word "pink." John Wycliffe used it in his translation of the biblical Book of Esther about 1382, and Chaucer used it a number of times in his writings, also in the late fourteenth century. By Shakespeare's time, in the late sixteenth century, both words also were used to describe blooming good health and flushed or blushing cheeks. "Rose-cheeked Laura, come," wrote Thomas Campion (*Laura*), who died in 1620. Shakespeare himself wrote, "Patience, thou young and rose-lipped cherubin" (*Othello*, 4:2), a usage still found in twentieth-century poetry;

A. E. Housman had it in one of his *Last Poems* (published in 1922): "Many a rose-lipt maiden, and many a lightfoot lad."

Poets also have been singularly fond of describing sunrise as *rosy*. Homer's oft-repeated *rosy-fingered dawn*, in translation, is legendary, and Edmund Spenser copied it in *The Faerie Queene* (published in 1596). John Milton, writing nearly a century later, dispensed with the fingers, a metaphor for the sun's rays: "Morn, all concerned without unrest, begins her rosy progress smiling" (*Paradise Lost*, Book XI, 1642–67).

> *I find earth not grey but rosy.*
>
> —ROBERT BROWNING,
> *At the "Mermaid"*

Milton anticipated a major modern meaning of *rosy*, that is, hopeful and optimistic. According to the *OED*, this usage dates from about 1775 and remains current. When we talk of a *rosy future*, we mean promising prospects.

These same positive connotations persist in *to come up roses* and *rose-colored glasses*. The first, which dates from the early 1900s, may have begun life as the second half of a less polite expression, "Fall into shit and come up roses," meaning to emerge unscathed from an unpleasant or difficult dilemma. A later variant, dating from about 1950, dispensed with the first half; *everything is coming up roses* simply means that everything is turning out very well, with the implication that this outcome is unexpected. Stephen Sondheim wrote a song, *Everything's Coming Up Roses*, for the musical *Gypsy* (1959; music by Jule Styne).

To see the world through *rose-colored glasses/spectacles* has been a metaphor since the 1850s for taking an optimistic, upbeat view of things. However, a study by two British physicians reported in 1990 in the *Journal of the Royal Society of Medicine* revealed that literally wearing colored glasses may mean quite the opposite. Wearers of tinted glasses, they found, displayed significantly higher levels of depression and psychosomatic illness, as well as other mental disorders, than those who wear clear glasses or none. The authors suggest that such individuals use colored glasses to hide their frailties.

These results, however, are far from conclusive—the study was small and may be culture-specific, individuals in America or other countries behaving quite differently—and the old metaphor for optimism is not likely to be revised.

Finally, *rosy* sometimes was a mispronunciation for French rosé wine, a pink table wine whose color is produced by removing the grape skins from the must before fermentation is complete. (In French the wine is called *vin rosé, rosé* meaning "pink.") Charles Dickens had it in *The Old Curiosity Shop* (1840–41): "Fan the sinking flame of hilarity with the wing of friendship; and pass the rosy." This usage probably has been obsolete for some time.

Born to the Purple

There was a certain rich man, which was clothed in purple and fine linen.

—Gospel of St. Luke (16:19)

*P*urple has been associated with royalty, or at least with royal garb, since ancient Roman times. Emperors, military commanders, and other high officials wore purple robes, making the color symbolic of power and wealth.

This association is actually quite odd, because the English word "purple" was a synonym for "red" or "crimson" until relatively recently. Hence, when King James's translators rendered the above-quoted passage, they really meant to describe a man dressed in sumptuous red.

The word "purple" comes from the Greek *porphúra*,

130

a species of shellfish that yielded, through an elaborate process, the dye called *Tyrian purple*. Very expensive to produce, it was reserved for special cloth and garments, such as those of kings. The color obtained was actually crimson, or at best a deep purplish red. In Old English this color was called *purpure*, and in Middle English *purpre* or *purper*, which finally became the modern word *purple*. It was, however, the color we now call crimson, and was associated with royalty, and a little later (in the fifteenth century) with ecclesiastical and royal mourning. It also was, to poets, the color of blood. Edmund Spenser described a flow of blood as "a large purple streame" (*The Faerie Queene*, 1596). Shakespeare subscribed to the same usage, describing "such purple teares" as were shed by a sword (*Henry VI*, Part 3, 5:6).

A similar confusion appears in the term *raised to the purple*, which is said of a priest who is raised to the rank of cardinal. The official color of cardinals is, of course, scarlet, but in the seventeenth century the word "purple" still served this purpose.

The term *born to the purple*, which means "of noble birth," and by extension, "of inherited wealth," further compounded the confusion. This term began life as born *in* the purple and referred to a custom of the Byzantine Empire whereby a special apartment was assigned to the empress for childbirth. Its walls were lined with porphyry, a hard, purplish-red rock, and the children born there were designated *porphyrogenite*. However, the Greek words for "porphyry" and "purple" are one and the same, so this word was translated as "purple-born" instead of "porphyry-born." The custom was explained in English, at first by John Selden in his *Titles of Honour* (1614), and later by Edward Gibbon in his very influential book, *The Decline and Fall of the Roman Empire* (1790). By then "purple" was used for the color so designated today—a mixture of blue and red. And despite the change of hue it remains associated with royalty. In mid-twentieth-century Britain there arose yet another term with this association, *purple airway*, denoting an air route reserved for aircraft carrying royal personages.

> *They may talk Freedom's airy*
> *Tell they're pupple in the face.*

> —JAMES RUSSELL LOWELL,
> *Biglow Papers* (1848)

Today, to be *purple in the face* betokens expending great effort, which is what Lowell meant here. In earlier times, however, it could mean the same variety of things now signified by RED IN THE FACE—being flushed with effort, emotion, embarrassment, glowing good health, intoxication. John Dryden thus described Bacchus, the god of wine and "sweet musician," as "flushed with a purple grace" (*Alexander's Feast*, 1697). In the eighteenth century William Wordsworth mixed his metaphors of color in *A Poet's Epitaph*:

> *Art thou a Man of purple cheer?*
> *A rosy Man, right plump to see?*

&ea; *Purple Prose* &ea;

Modern editors and writers tend to frown on *purple patches*, the name long given to brilliant and ornate passages in an otherwise ordinary piece of writing. They regard them as ostentatious, gaudy, and best avoided. The term for such writing has been around for nearly 2,000 years, for it comes from the Latin writer Horace, who in his *De Arte poetica* wrote, "Often a purple patch or two is tacked on to a serious work of high promise, to give an effect of color."

Not everyone agrees that this practice is so bad, and

indeed Paul West wrote a piece called *In Defense of Purple Prose*, where he held that it can intensify description and show off the expansive or creative powers of the human mind (*The New York Times*, 1985). The more common view, however, was expressed by the English critic and editor Cyril Connolly in his autobiography, *Enemies of Promise* (1938). There he ruefully admitted, "When I write after dark the shades of evening scatter their purple through my prose."

Purple Heart

In 1782 George Washington instituted the practice of awarding a medal to soldiers who were wounded while on active duty. It consisted of a small, heart-shaped piece of purple cloth, but it was abandoned after the end of the Revolutionary War. In 1932, however, the U.S. Army reinstated the practice. This medal, called the *Purple Heart*, consists of a silver heart bearing a picture of Washington that is suspended from a white-edged purple ribbon.

The name *purple heart* has two other, quite unrelated meanings. The plum-colored wood of a large tropical Western Hemisphere tree, of the genus *Copaifera*, is also known as purple heart or purple wood. Also, "purple heart" is slang for a stimulant, Drinamyl (dexamphetamine), so called for the shape and color of the pills.

Deep Purple

The color purple is not officially in the spectrum. That position is taken by the color *violet*, about which more later. But purple does appear in nature, particularly in sunrises and sunsets. Harriet Beecher Stowe (1811–96) had it in her poem *Still, Still with Thee*: "Still, still with

Thee, when purple morning breaketh." John Greenleaf Whittier similarly described, in his *The Last Walk in Autumn*, the "purple lights on Alpine snow." More recently, the purple of dusk became the subject of the popular song, "Deep Purple," with music by Peter de Rose and lyrics by W. Mitchell Parish. Published in 1939, it became immensely popular. Baseball immortal Babe Ruth (1895–1948) was reportedly so fond of it that he had it performed on each of his last ten birthdays.

A few decades later the name Deep Purple was adopted by a hard rock group that became as popular among teenagers of the 1970s as its namesake had been with their parents. It still was in existence as late as 1991 but was then described by critic Jim Sullivan as "a former powerhouse of a band that seemed, mostly, plodding and irrelevant" (*The Boston Globe*, April 3, 1991).

The distant mountains often have a purple glow, imparted by the sun. Their aspect inspired Katharine Lee Bates to write the poem *America the Beautiful* (1893), whose opening lines actually were written on the summit of Pikes Peak in Colorado: "O beautiful for spacious skies, for amber waves of grain, For purple mounted majesties above the fruited plain." Set to music that had been composed earlier by Samuel Augustus Ward (in 1882), it became one of America's standard patriotic songs.

Other than sky and mountains, and very occasionally the sea, the principal objects in nature identified as purple are vegetable—that is, flowers and fruits. There are few purple animals, other than a handful of birds, fish, and insects, among them the *purple admiral*, an outstanding large butterfly. As for mammals, Gelett Burgess put it most memorably in a poem first published in the *San Francisco Lark*, which he edited from 1895 to 1897:

> *I never saw a purple Cow,*
> *I never hope to see one;*
> *But I can tell you, anyhow,*
> *I'd rather see than be one.*

Purple as a plum is one of the few similes involving this color (in contrast to the dozens for black, white, red, etc.). Different shades of purple tend to be distinguished by the names of plants they resemble—*heliotrope*; the aforementioned *plum*; *grape*; *lavender*; and, of course, *violet*.

The word "violet" has been used since the fourteenth century for both the color, generally described as purplish or reddish blue, and for the flower. Violet is at the opposite end of the visible spectrum from red. In folklore violet is, like purple, symbolic of authority and of mourning. In Christianity violet symbolizes humility, penitence, and suffering, and is used in church decorations during Advent and Lent.

References to violet generally allude to the flower rather than the color. A major exception is *ultraviolet*, the name given to radiation beyond the violet in the spectrum, with a wavelength shorter than that of violet light. Ultraviolet has been so called only since about 1870; prior to that, from its discovery about 1840 until 1870, it was known as *lavender rays*.

⤫ *Shades of Purple* ⤫

Two other shades of purple derive their names from the French for a plant and an insect, respectively, and two others are named for bloody battles of the nineteenth century. The color *mauve* is named for a bright, delicate purple dye derived from a coal-tar aniline discovered in 1856, the first of many coal-tar dyes. Its name comes from the French for mallow, a large family of plants with big, showy flowers, often purple in color, including the hibiscus, hollyhock, and rose of Sharon. From this also came the term *mauve decade* for the 1890s, a period characterized by prosperous complacency.

The color *puce*, a brownish purple, derives its name from the French word for flea and has been so called since the late eighteenth century.

Magenta, a brilliant purplish red, is named for a famous battle at the Italian town of Magenta, where in 1859 the Austrians were defeated by a combined force of Sardinians and French troops. The aniline dye of this color was discovered later that year and named to commemorate the exceptionally bloody battle. In the same year another aniline dye was discovered, this one more bluish pink in hue, and it was named *solferino*, for the other great battle of the same campaign, at the town of Solferino.

Seeing Red

*T*he color red has been so called in English since about A.D. 900. It is the primary color at the lower or least refracted end of the spectrum, but its name is used for shades ranging from very bright red, also called *scarlet* or *crimson*, to reddish yellow or reddish brown (the color of the *red fox*, for example).

Today red is symbolically associated with anarchy and revolution (see BETTER RED THAN DEAD below), but in earlier times it was an establishment color—the color of royal livery (where it was sometimes called purple; see under BORN TO THE PURPLE for further explanation). For this reason it also became the color of formal hunting clothes—after all, King Henry II had declared fox hunting to be a royal sport—but there it was known as HUNTING PINKS.

In Christian ecclesiastical circles red stood for martyrdom. In heraldry it has two names: *gules*, which symbolizes magnanimity; and *sanguine*, standing for fortitude. The Irish poet William Butler Yeats pointed out that in fairy tales the caps of fairies and of musicians are always red (also see REDCAP below), and in folklore red stood for magic, as well as for vigorous action, anger, blood, and the like.

🪶 *Red as a Beet* 🪶

The similes involving red are manifold. Among the oldest are *red as blood*, whence also *blood-red*, and *red as a rose*. Chaucer used both of these in the late fourteenth century, and they were far from new even then. Chaucer also used *red as a fox*, which seems more open to dispute. His contemporary, William Langland (author of *Piers Ploughman*), had *red as any glede*, "glede" being a now obsolete word for "live coal" but still a valid comparison. "Red as" various fruits and flowers also was (and continues to be)

very common. Besides the rose we have *red as a geranium, carnation, peony,* and *poppy,* as well as *red as a cherry, apple,* and *currant wine.* The most popular comparisons from the animal world are *red as a cock's* (or *turkey's*) *comb* and *red as a lobster.*

Interestingly enough, some of these comparisons are flattering and others are not. To be red as a beet or a lobster generally betokens flushing from physical effort or sunburn or acute embarrassment (also see MY FACE IS RED below). But lips as red as a cherry or cheeks as red as an apple signify beauty, at least according to makers of lipstick and rouge. Certainly that is what Robert Burns meant with:

> *Oh, my Luve's like a red red rose*
> *That's newly sprung in June.*

On the other hand, his near-contemporary, Charles Stearns, disagreed (*The Ladies' Philosophy of Love,* 1797):

> *The flaming red denotes a callous mind,*
> *Too harsh for love, or sentiment refined.*

‏ My Face Is Red ‏

As suggested above, being red in the face can signify any of a number of conditions: the blush of shame or embarrassment; extreme physical exertion; or violent anger. "Blushing is the color of virtue," claimed the Greek philosopher Diogenes (fourth century B.C.), the very one who allegedly searched the whole world for a virtuous woman. He presumably meant blushing from embarrassment, as does the old Portuguese proverb "Better a red face than a black heart."

Physiologically a blush, whatever the cause, occurs in exactly the same way—that is, rapidly increased di-

lation of the blood vessels enables increased blood flow to the skin of the face. Although the effect is the same whether it results from vigorously blowing a trumpet, being caught shoplifting, or being warmly praised, we use slightly varying terms that do suggest different causes. *"My face is red"* is usually uttered by a person who is admitting acute embarrassment owing to a mistake or misdeed. *"You can try until you're red in the face,"* on the other hand, means you can exert yourself to the utmost (for all the good it will do).

Further, a red face may or may not be considered attractive, depending on just what part of the face is affected. As noted before, *red cheeks* and *red lips* are just fine, indicating good health and physical beauty. Chaucer's Sir Thopas had "lippes rede as rose," and Elizabethan poets all tended to extol this trait in their love poems. "He that loves a rosy cheek, Or a coral lip admires," wrote Thomas Carew (*Disdain Returned*), and "Her lips were red," rhapsodized John Suckling (*Upon a Wedding*). A *red nose*, on the other hand, has long indi-

cated a certain coarseness, as well as alcoholic overindulgence. In Shakespeare's song about the icy winds of
winter, "Marion's nose looks red and raw" (*Love's Labour's Lost*, 5:2). Four centuries later the tale of *Rudolph,
the Red-Nosed Reindeer*, with his embarrassingly shiny
red nose, is completely understandable to children.

The same is true of *red eyes*, whether bloodshot from
weeping, a usage current since the fourteenth century,
or from too much liquor. "Amyas was pacing the deck
. . . his eyes red with rage and weeping," wrote Charles
Kingsley (*Westward Ho!*, 1855). The association with alcoholic overindulgence gave rise to the colloquial American use of *red-eye* for raw whiskey, dating from the early
nineteenth century. "We had to treat to 'red-eye' or 'rot-
gut,' as whiskey is here called," wrote John A. Quitman
(*Life*, 1819). Later, in the second half of the twentieth
century, another cause of bloodshot eyes, sleeplessness,
gave rise to a second meaning for *red-eye*, an overnight
coast-to-coast flight. This American colloquialism has
been around since about 1965. Lady Bird Johnson mentioned it in a *White House Diary* entry of 1968: "Lynda
was coming in on the 'red-eye special' from California
about 7 A.M."

🔊 *The Red-headed League* 🔊

*All red-headed men who are sound in body and
mind and above the age of 21 years are eligible.
Apply in person.*

—ARTHUR CONAN DOYLE,
The Red-headed League

Arthur Conan Doyle knew what he was about when he
picked red hair as an operative part of the plot (and title)
of this famous Sherlock Holmes mystery about a bank

robbery. Red hair is much rarer than blond or brown, and consequently stands out. Red-headed and/or red-bearded men were singled out very early on, even being named for this trait. Examples include *Eric the Red*, Norse explorer and colonizer of Greenland (c. A.D. 985) and *William the Red*, or William II of England (c. 1056–1100).

Similarly, its distinctiveness made people consider red hair indicative of various personality characteristics. For centuries it was regarded as a sign of lewdness and deceit, and even today it is frequently associated with a hot temper. "Beware of red men," wrote John Florio (*Second Frutes*, 1591), warning that they are not to be trusted. One source claims that this view applied only to red-haired men and not to women, and that it came from the fact that Judas Iscariot, who betrayed Jesus, had red hair. Not everyone agreed, however. David Ferguson's collection *Scottish Proverbs* (c. 1595) has, "To a Red man rede thy Reade [reveal your intentions] . . ." for "Red is wise." And Thomas Fuller (*Gnomologia*, 1732) made a fine distinction: "He is false by Nature that has a black Head and a red Beard."

In the late sixteenth and early seventeenth centuries, fat taken from the corpse of a red-headed person was valued as an ingredient for poison. The practice is mentioned in several plays from this period, among them Thomas Middleton's *The Witch* and George Chapman's *Bussy d'Ambois* (cited by Dr. Ebenezer Brewer).

In late nineteenth-century America, *red-headed* was a synonym for "impetuous." A *Congressional Record* entry from 1900 records a statement by Representative J. G. Cannon of Illinois chiding a fellow congressman, "We are dealing with a question which merits the most careful consideration; but you are 'red-headed,' and nothing that we do, or fail to do, suits you."

❧ *Caught Red-handed* ❧

Thanks to Sherlock Holmes's perspicacity, the would-be bank robbers in Arthur Conan Doyle's story were caught *red-handed*. This term for being apprehended in the act of committing a crime has been around since the first half of the nineteenth century. It was also used earlier but then denoted a more serious crime, signifying that one had been caught with blood (someone else's) on one's hands—in other words, in the act of murder.

The connection between red and blood was, of course, made long ago. "Strong wyn, reed as blood," wrote Chaucer in the Prologue to his *Canterbury Tales*. The differentiation of types of blood cell came much later; only in 1846 were *red blood cells* or *corpuscles* first cited in the literature. By 1881, however, the term *red-blooded* had another meaning as well, that of being vigorous and virile, and it continues to be used in this sense. Edgar Rice Burroughs had it in his popular jungle thriller *Tarzan of the Apes* (1914): "Tarzan . . . did what no red-blooded man needs a lesson in doing."

Sherlock Holmes also was adept at avoiding the *red herrings* strewn in his path. Since the late nineteenth century this term has been used to signify any kind of diversion. It came from the literal use of a smoked herring, which turns from gray to reddish brown during smoking and acquires a strong odor. At first a red herring was used to train hunting dogs to follow a scent; later it was sometimes useful in throwing hounds *off* the scent of an escaping criminal.

In the twentieth century "red herring" acquired still another meaning. In the securities industry, a red herring is a preliminary prospectus for a new issue, given to brokers to attract buyers at the outset but bearing an inscription, in red print (hence the name), that the information it contains is subject to change. It does not attempt to divert or mislead but merely indicates that it does not constitute a firm offer at this time.

❧ *Another Redskin Bit the Dust* ❧

The early European settlers called the North American Indians, with their copper-colored skin, *Red Indians, red men,* or *redskins.* James Fenimore Cooper (1789–1851) was the first writer to take them up as a new subject of fiction and became famous for his romanticized portrayal of the Indian as a "noble savage." In his *The Last of the Mohicans* and other popular novels, Indians were "redskins" and white characters were "palefaces."

However, it was the popular novelists of the late nineteenth century who exploited the cowboys-and-Indians subject to the fullest. In their improbable sagas, the Indians were generally villains to be downed by the courageous cowboys, one by one. In the Western novels of Edward Z. C. Judson (1822–86), who wrote as Ned Buntline, as well as in the dozens of dime novels in the Nick Carter series, which appeared from the 1880s to the 1920s, "Another redskin bit the dust" was the standard announcement whenever the hero's pistol "spoke." The genre was extolled by Quincy Kilby (1854–1931) in his poem *And Seven More Redskins Bit the Dust*:

> *Here in my library I sit,*
> *Amid rare volumes richly bound . . .*
> *Their weakness fills me with disgust,*
> *I want that crude, hard-fisted tale,*
> *Where* seven more redskins bit the dust.

Today the term "redskin" for a native American is considered pejorative and demeaning, at least when applied to actual Indians. It survives, however, in the National

Football League's famous team, the Washington (D.C.)
Redskins.

❧ *Let's Paint the Town Red!* ❧

It's a *red-letter day* when the *rednecks* come to town, sick
of *red-flannel hash* but eager for *red meat*, washed down
with *dago red* or *red-eye*, listening to music by some *red-
hot mama*, and looking for a *scarlet woman* in the *red-
light district*.

Most of these terms come from late nineteenth- and
early twentieth-century America. Dealing first with the
exceptions, a *red-letter day* comes from the Middle Ages,
when the dates for saints' and feast days on church calendars often were inscribed in red. By the early eighteenth century the meaning had been extended to any
kind of a special day or even a lucky day. Charles Lamb
used it in describing the dullness of Oxford during the

DINE *and* **DANCE**

long vacation: "The red-letter days now become, to all
intents, dead-letter days" (*Essays of Elia*, 1823).

The expression *scarlet woman* has an even older
source, the biblical Book of Revelation (17:6), in which
St. John saw her as a vision. She had an inscription on
her forehead, "Mystery, Babylon the Great, the mother
of harlots and abominations of the earth." Interpreters
of this mysterious book generally believe that the scarlet
woman represented Rome, drunk with the blood of saints,
but later the term came to be used more loosely for a
whore or other sinful woman.

In the early nineteenth century *redneck* was a name
for Presbyterians in Fayetteville, Arkansas, according to
A. Royall (*Southern Tour*, 1830; cited by the *OED*). That
appellation has long been obsolete, but in the late nineteenth century the term began to be used in the American
South, mostly by the well-to-do, for the poor white in-
habitants of rural areas. Many of them were tenant farmers who worked the very infertile red clay soil of the hills
behind the rich delta lands. The term, which probably
alludes to their sunburned necks, was used scornfully
then, and it still is. Today it refers not only to rural white
laborers, usually but not always southerners, but also to
the crude and racist attitudes ascribed to this group.

Red flannel underwear was common attire for laborers and others in the United States from the mid-
nineteenth century on. The term *red-flannel hash*, which
comes from the fabric, denotes a variation on hash made
from leftover corned beef. The term is recorded in *Dialect
Notes* in 1907 and refers to the appearance of hash when
chopped cooked beets are added to the traditional meat-
and-potatoes mixture. *Red meat*, on the other hand,
means any meat that is dark red in color before being
cooked, particularly beef. The term, which contrasts it to
the WHITE MEAT of poultry, has been in use since the late
nineteenth century. Since about 1970, vegetarians and
health-conscious individuals in general have brought the

term to widespread public attention, warning that the high fat and cholesterol content of red meat poses a health hazard, so it should be consumed in great moderation (if at all). However, *red-blooded Americans* pride themselves on ignoring such warnings and continue to consume it with gusto.

To paint the town red has meant to indulge in spirited carousing, generally involving heavy drinking, since the late nineteenth century. The term appeared in the *Boston Journal* (1884): "Whenever there was any excitement or anybody got particularly loud, they always said somebody was 'painting the town red.' "

Indulging in *red-eye*, or raw whiskey, had been mentioned since the early nineteenth century. Two newer terms for an alcoholic beverage are *dago red* and *red ink*, both meaning cheap red wine. The former employs the offensive appellation "dago" for those of Italian ancestry, who are indeed famous for red vintages of high as well as poor quality. The term has been around since about 1900. The synonym "red ink," first recorded about 1919, also has another meaning (see IN THE RED below).

The description *red-hot* has meant literally glowing with heat since the fourteenth century and has been applied to individuals of a fiery or passionate temperament since about 1600. In the 1920s the style of jazz played by small bands, such as those of Louis Armstrong and Eddie Condon, was called *hot jazz*, as opposed to the smoother, danceable swing music of the big bands. Some of the women singers associated with hot jazz bands came to be called *red-hot mamas*. A 1935 piece in *Time* magazine described Sophie Tucker (1884–1966) as "the last of the red-hot mamas."

The use of a *red light* as a traffic signal to stop dates from the early days of railroading, in the mid-nineteenth century, and soon was extended to signal any kind of warning of danger (much later it sometimes was called a *red alert*). Late in the nineteenth century, brothels be-

gan to display a red light at their front door, presumably
to signal passersby to stop and patronize them. From this
practice came the term *red-light district* for the section
of a town where many houses of prostitution are located.

Red light also is the name of a children's game in
which the players must stop running toward a goal when
one of them, selected as "It," calls out "Red light."

Railroading also contributed, in the 1920s, the term
red ball express for a fast freight train. During World
War II this term gained currency as the name for a one-
way high-speed column of Allied trucks bringing supplies
to the front.

🙣 *The Red Badge of Courage* 🙣

Red also is closely associated with war and bloodshed. It
was the color of Mars, the Roman god of war, and the
planet named for him was originally so called because of
its reddish tinge.

The term *redcoats*, as the British Army long was
known, dates from the seventeenth century, when Oliver
Cromwell introduced a red uniform for the line regiments
of his New Model Army. It probably was not the first use
of red uniforms—an early sixteenth-century ballad, *Lady
Bessy*, contains the line, "Sir William Standley . . . ten
thousand read coates had he," which almost certainly
refers to a troop (and not his personal wardrobe). On April
18, 1775, when General Thomas Gage sent 700 men to
Concord, Massachusetts, to seize military stores being
gathered there by the colonists, Paul Revere, William
Dawes, and Samuel Prescott rode all night to warn the
colonists, "The redcoats are coming! The redcoats are
coming!"

On October 25, 1854, when the British were engaged
in the Crimean War, the *thin red line* of their infantry
made history at the Battle of Balaclava. As the result of

an error, the Earl of Cardigan led an English light cavalry brigade in a hopeless charge on a heavily armed
Russian position, in which more than one-third of his men
were killed or wounded. (This was the famous charge of
the light brigade.) They were backed up by infantry,
which was later described by several correspondents, including Sir William Howard Russell, who gave this account: "[The Russians] dash on towards that thin red line
tipped with steel" (*The British Expedition to the Crimea*,
1877). Kipling wrote about it as well: "It's 'thin red line
of 'eroes' when drums begin to roll" (*Tommy*), and the
Scottish artist Robert Gibb painted a picture called *The
Thin Red Line*, exhibited at the Royal Scottish Academy
Exposition of 1881. The British uniform was converted
to khaki in the Boer War (1899–1901), but "redcoats" has
a permanent place in history, and "thin red line" appeared in a 1991 *New York Times* headline, "The Thin
Red Line—Gorbachev Fails to Stop the Forces He Set in
Motion," where it is a metaphor for the Russian leader's
unpopular brand of communism.

Stephen Crane's novel *The Red Badge of Courage*
(1895) concerns the American Civil War, and the "red"
badge" here refers to a bloody war wound as well as re-
calling the folk symbolism of a red badge standing for
courage. It is a stirring account of a recruit under fire,
particularly remarkable in view of the fact that Crane
himself had never been on a battlefront.

A more lighthearted use of martial red is *Curse you,
Red Baron!* This exclamation comes from Charles M.
Schulz's comic strip *Peanuts*, in which the beagle Snoopy
periodically indulges in the fantasy of being a World War
I fighter ace. However, his dream invariably ends rudely
as he falls victim to the (real-life) German ace Baron
Manfred von Richthofen (1892–1918), who always flew
in a red aircraft. Von Richthofen was credited with shooting down eighty airplanes and was himself killed in action on April 21, 1918.

❧ *Red, White, and Blue* ❧

Since 1777 Americans have tended to associate *red, white, and blue* with their flag, the Stars and Stripes, whose "white is for purity; red for valor; and blue for justice" (Charles Sumner, *Are We A Nation?*, 1867). Britons, on the other hand, associate it with the United Kingdom's flag, the Union Jack, approximately a century older than the American. Or, as D. T. Shaw put it (*Britannia, Pride of Ocean*, 1855):

> *May the Service United ne'er sever,*
> *And both to their Colours prove true,*
> *The Army and Navy for ever!*
> *Three cheers for the Red, White and Blue!*

These English-speaking nations are not, of course, unique in their choice of national flag colors. The French tricolor, used from the time of the French Revolution, is also red, white, and blue, as are the flags of dozens of other countries on all of the world's continents. In the United States, however, the term *red, white, and blue* always conjures up the image of the American flag, and by extension, patriotism.

❧ *Red Flags, Shirts, and Caps* ❧

A plain *red flag*, on the other hand, has been a symbol of battle since the early seventeenth century and of defiance and revolution since the early eighteenth century. Some authorities say it was used as a call to arms in the time of the Roman Empire. It was used during the French Revolution by the *républicains rouges* (*Red Republicans*), the most violent of the extremists, who also wore red caps.

Half a century later, in 1848, France's new republican government, the Second Republic, was also known as the *Red Republic* and was regarded as quite radical. During this era the Italian revolutionaries were known as the *Red Shirts*, which they in fact wore. In 1843 the Italian patriot Giuseppe Garibaldi, who had fled to South America to escape arrest after taking part in an unsuccessful republican plot, was raising an army in Uruguay, then involved in a bloody civil war. At this time, as the result of a trade war with Argentina, a glut of red woolen shirts came on the market. The Uruguay government bought them at a very low price and gave them to Garibaldi for his men. In 1848, when revolution swept over Europe, Garibaldi and his followers returned, bringing their red shirts with them, and acquired the name Red Shirts, which later was extended to any revolutionary group.

In mid-twentieth-century America the term took on a completely different meaning. It was used for a college athlete, usually an injured football player, who stays in college for an extra year and practices with but does not play on a varsity team, because the rules permit one to play only a total of four years as a nonprofessional. The name comes from the fact that these men traditionally wore red shirts on the field to distinguish themselves from the varsity players.

❧ *Better Red Than Dead* ❧

In the late nineteenth century the Russian Communists adopted a red flag as the symbol of international socialism, and in 1889 *The Red Flag*, a socialist song by James Connell, was published. For all of the twentieth century, *Red* has meant Communist or Communist sympathizer to most people in most contexts. The term *Red Army* meant at first the troops of the Bolsheviks, and after 1918 those of the Soviet Union.

Following the victory of the Communists in the Russian Revolution of 1917, many countries feared that communism would supersede their own governments and ideologies, and in fact it was the stated Communist aim to take over the entire world. This potential expansion came to be called *the Red menace*. B. Coan had it in *Red Web* (1925): "It is time, right now, to get down to cases about this thing we hear called the 'red menace.' " It gave rise to widespread fear, the so-called *Red scare*, which in turn prompted *Red-baiting*, the harassment of known or suspected Communists. Red-baiting began in the late 1920s and culminated in America in the hearings conducted by Senator Joseph McCarthy in the early 1950s. The slogan of ultraconservative Americans at this time was *Better dead than Red*—that is, living under communism would be a fate worse than death. This slogan later was turned around by the nuclear disarmament movement in Britain, which, denouncing the arms race between East and West, proclaimed, *Better Red than dead*—that is, better let the Soviets win than have us all be annihilated in a nuclear war.

In the first half of the twentieth century "Red" for

"Communist" referred primarily to Russian communism and its supporters. By midcentury, however, the term was being used for communism elsewhere. Thus the popular name for the Communist People's Republic of China had become *Red China*. In the 1960s a particularly militant group of Chinese Communists who supported the policies of Mao Zedong were called, in English, *the Red Guard*. A decade later, a radical group of terrorists in Italy was called *the Red Brigade*. These last two terms illustrate the present trend of using *Red* mainly to describe leftist extremism of any kind, anywhere, without necessarily being attached to a particular government or political doctrine.

🙖 *The Red Cross* 🙖

The Battle of Solferino, which gave us the color called SOLFERINO, was also responsible for the birth of the *Red Cross*, an international organization founded to alleviate human suffering and promote public health.

In 1862 a Swiss, Jean Henry Dunant, wrote an account of the battle in which he described the sufferings of the wounded and urged that voluntary agencies be formed to help war victims. He also asked that medical services to the war wounded be considered neutral. As a result, an international conference was convened in 1864. It was attended by sixteen nations, most of whom signed the Geneva Convention, which provided for the neutrality of those providing medical services in wartime. In Dunant's honor a reverse of the Swiss flag, a *red cross* on a white background, was chosen as the official emblem to mark personnel and supplies engaged in such humanitarian missions. Since then, the International Red Cross has grown into a huge organization that has played an important role in many areas, from providing war relief in conflicts all over the world to subsidizing blood drives and other public health programs. In some non-Christian countries its emblem is replaced by a red crescent (in Iran by a red lion and sun).

The symbol of the red cross antedates the modern organization by many centuries. It was the emblem of St. George, a Crusader said to have been a hero at Antioch in 1098 and the patron saint of England. In Edmund Spenser's *The Faerie Queene* (1596), a long epic poem in which the moral virtues are treated allegorically, the *Red Cross Knight* is the personification of St. George, who is sent to destroy the evil dragon.

🦋 *Seeing Red* 🦋

Describing a new biography of former First Lady Nancy Reagan, *Publishers Weekly* said, "Ronnie's wife will no doubt be seeing (as well as wearing) red next May when she gets her hands on Kitty Kelley's next 'character study'" (November 23, 1990). The writer in passing had alluded to Mrs. Reagan's love for red clothes, as well as to anticipating her fury at a less than flattering portrayal.

Since about 1900, *seeing red* has meant becoming extremely angry. It is primarily an Americanism, and no one knows exactly how it originated. Some authorities believe it alludes to the red cape waved by the matador to anger a bull (see also RED RAG below), but there is no verification for this theory. Most likely the expression reflects the long-standing association of red with blood, heat, and fire, in turn associated with passion and anger.

> *He that commeth before an Elephant*
> *will not wear bright colours, nor*
> *he that commeth to a Bull red.*
>
> —JOHN LYLY,
> *Euphues and His England* (1580)

A piece of red cloth, or *red rag*, has been regarded as an irritant ever since the sixteenth century, and perhaps even earlier. Bullfighters traditionally use a red-lined cape to arouse the bull, but they know full well that it is the movement of the cape, and not the color, that causes the animal to charge. Nevertheless, we still describe something calculated to enrage as being *like a red rag to a bull*. Ancient folk superstition also claimed a red cloth would ward off the evil eye and/or enhance magic, and perhaps this belief underlies the bullfighting myth.

The term *red rag* also is an old (seventeenth-century) slang term for the tongue. John Wolcot (also known as Peter Pindar) uses it in one of his odes (1783):

> *Discovering in his mouth a tongue,*
> *He must not his palaver balk;*
> *So keeps it running all day long,*
> *And fancies his red rag can talk.*

Although this term is still listed in Eric Partridge's *Dictionary of the Underworld* of 1950, it is seldom heard nowadays, at least not in America.

?❧ *Little Red Riding Hood* ?❧

Some other items of red fabric are part of our language. A *red ribbon*, for example, is a common award for coming in second in a race or other competition (exceeded, of course, by the BLUE RIBBON for first place). A *red hat* has signified the office of Cardinal since the sixteenth century, when these churchmen were given a flat, broad-rimmed red hat that became synonymous with their position. "The King hath bought half the College of Redhats," wrote Tennyson in 1884 (*Becket*, 2:2).

Although the headgear has changed, a visiting Cardinal would no doubt be accorded *red carpet* treatment, at least in some circles. His hosts may or may not actually roll out a red carpet to welcome him, the practice that is the source of this term. The expression dates from the early twentieth century; the custom is surely much older. A 1991 *New York Times* article about changes in train service showed a photo of a red carpet being rolled out in 1948 at New York's Grand Central Station for passengers using a long-distance train, the *20th Century Limited*.

A *redcap*, on the other hand, could expect no such treatment, although in this day of waning personal services he might well be entitled to a comparable welcome. In America a redcap is a railroad porter and has been so called, after the headgear of his uniform, since the early twentieth century. However, the term has been around for four centuries in Britain, where it signifies the less welcome presence of military police (who wear red covers over their caps). In folklore a red cap also is the badge of fairies, and in the seventeenth century the phrase "You shall have the red cap" was said to a marriage broker (according to John Ray's proverb collection of 1678).

The story of Little Red Riding Hood and her visit to the wolf disguised as the child's grandmother is one of the most familiar in the Grimm brothers' collection. The hooded red cloak of the story became a popular clothing item in the early twentieth century and in fact was called a *red riding hood*. This usage is probably obsolete, although the tale remains popular.

🐦 *The Red Sea* 🐦

*And Moses stretched out his hand over the sea;
and the Lord caused the sea to go back by a strong
east wind all that night, and made the sea dry
land, and the waters were divided.*

—Book of Exodus, 14:21

When Moses was leading the Israelites out of Egypt, God parted the sea waters to let them through and then closed them again so that the pursuing Egyptians were drowned. Through this biblical story, the *Red Sea*, which is the one described, became the symbol of salvation and spiritual deliverance.

No one knows exactly why the Red Sea is so called. The English traveler Sir John Maundeville, who was not known for great accuracy, wrote (c. 1400), "In some places thereof is the Gravelle reede [red]: and therefore Men clepen [call] it the Rede Sea." The name is very old. The Romans already called it *Mare Rubrum*, a name they took from the Greeks, who translated it from the Hebrew. Possibly it comes from coral in its bed, or from the reflection of the eastern sky in its waters.

Modern scientists suggest the name may come from the presence of red algae on the water's surface. Such organisms are also known as *the red tide*, a name used in America since about 1900 for the proliferation of these microscopic brownish-red creatures, mostly dinoflagellates (in Britain it is called *red water*). Some species produce a highly toxic substance that accumulates in the tissues of shellfish, which become poisonous to human beings and other animals who eat them.

Algae also cause the phenomenon known since the late seventeenth century as *red snow*. The particular species responsible is *Protococcus nivalis*, and it is common in both arctic and alpine regions. In earlier times it was regarded as a portent of evil; today it is recognized as harmless.

❧ *Red Sky at Night* ❧

When it is evening, ye say, it will be fair weather: for the sky is red.

—Book of Matthew, 16:2–3

The phenomenon of a red sunset preceding fair weather, and its corollary, a red sunrise preceding rainy weather, was observed by the ancients. Versions of "Red sky at night, sailor's delight; red sky in the morning, sailors take warning" appear in practically every proverb collection ever made, in English ones from the 1550s on. Moreover, there is scientific evidence for this empirical observation, according to meteorologist Fred Gadomski of Pennsylvania State University (quoted in *The New York Times*, November 20, 1990).

Both sunrise and sunset are reddish normally because of what happens to sunlight traveling through the atmosphere at a low angle. Most colors of the spectrum are scattered away, so that only the reddish hues remain. However, by looking at the part of the sky where the sun isn't—eastward at night and westward in the morning —some rough weather prediction can be made. Sunlight interacting with additional water vapor in that part of the sky creates red and orange hues. Therefore a red sky in the west in the morning means that a storm system creating these hues is coming in. On the other hand, a red sky in the east at night shows that the storm system or moisture is moving away.

The evening sky is responsible for *Red Sails in the Sunset*, an English popular song of 1935, with lyrics by Jimmy Kennedy and music by Will Grosz, that became an enormous hit in the United States. Its title presumably is the source of the slang term *red sails in the sunset*, meaning that a woman is menstruating and therefore is not available for sexual intercourse. (According to Eric Partridge, the Australians use the same term as a sarcastic reference to oversentimentality.)

Astronomers characterize a kind of star as a *red dwarf*, a name first used about 1915 and based on its reddish color and low surface temperature. They also invented the term *red shift*, for a shift toward longer wavelengths of an object's spectral lines, caused by its movement away from the earth.

"Astronomers Looking to See Red," a *Boston Globe* headline proclaimed (March 25, 1991). They were not seeking a reason for losing their tempers (see SEEING RED above) but were announcing plans to develop telescopes that could "see" *infrared light* and proclaimed that the 1990s would be the decade of infrared astronomy.

Infrared is the part of the spectrum beyond red (*infra* means "below"). Red is visible, but infrared is not. It is analogous to ULTRAVIOLET, which lies at the opposite end of the spectrum, beyond violet. The name has been in use since the 1820s, half a century longer than ultraviolet, so called only since about 1870. Infrared radiation penetrates readily through space but cannot penetrate the earth's atmosphere because it is absorbed by water vapor before it can get through. Therefore it has been poorly explored, compared to other kinds of radiation. The development of more specialized telescopes and their placement in orbiting satellites is expected to "see" infrared and consequently answer some vital questions concerning the evolution of distant solar systems as well as our own.

❧ *In the Red* ❧

Heavy betting on *the red and the black* may land you *in the red*—that is, without a *red cent* to your name. The first term, referring to the gambling game of roulette, and also to a variety of poker, has been around since the early nineteenth century (in English). William Thackeray wrote, "A confounded run on the red had finished him" (*Pendennis*, 1849).

The expression *in the red*, for being in debt or bankrupt, has been used only since the early 1900s, and was joined by *red ink* in the 1920s. Both are derived from the bookkeeping practice of marking debits in red pencil or ink and credits in black. Although computers are rapidly replacing manual entries of this kind, the terms remain current.

The expression *red cent* is an early nineteenth-century Americanism derived from the fact that pennies or cent coins in those days were made of copper and consequently were reddish in color. Because the cent is also the denomination of least value, the term was generally used contemptuously or negatively. "It would not have cost you a red cent," wrote J. S. Jones (*People's Lawyer*, 1839; cited by the *OED*).

🍋 *Under the Rubric of Red Tape* 🍋

The word *rubric* comes from the Latin *rubrica*, for red ocher or vermilion. The ancient Romans called a law a rubric because it was written in red. Similarly, the term was extended to directions for administering the sacraments—for example, in liturgical books—because these, too, were inscribed in red. Today, however, we use the word more loosely, for an established mode of conduct or an explanation or a category.

The term *red tape* is much newer. In Great Britain from the seventeenth century or so, legal papers and official reports were often bound with a red ribbon or tape, and by extension this term came to mean the intricacies and delays of legal and other official processes and bureaucracies. The *OED* cites a use of the term in 1736, in a poem by Lord Hervey (1693–1743), but it became widespread only in the mid-nineteenth century, used by such writers as Charles Dickens and Thomas Carlyle. The latter is said to have popularized it; he used it in the same pamphlet in which he characterized economics as a Dismal Science (*Latter-Day Pamphlets No. 1: The Present Time*), as well as elsewhere.

Although use of a *red pencil* to correct school papers and other written work surely antedates employment of this term as a verb, it is not so recorded until 1959 or so. (Also see BLUE PENCIL.)

The term *redlining* is newer still, coming into use in America only in the 1970s. It refers to the practice whereby banks and other lending institutions arbitrarily exclude certain classes of borrower. A figurative "red line" is drawn around certain neighborhoods on a city map—usually around both poor and largely minority-inhabited neighborhoods—and the banks either refuse to lend to residents of those areas or do so only on premium terms. In the United States the practice was outlawed by the Community Reinvestment Act of 1977 but persists nevertheless. Originally applied only to real-estate loans, redlining now may refer to almost any kind of investment policy whereby certain categories are systematically excluded.

Another kind of snobbishness is at the heart of the term *redbrick*, used in Britain since the late nineteenth century for any university located in a large industrial city. It evolved, of course, to distinguish such schools from Cambridge and Oxford, venerable institutions located in beautiful old cities and associated for centuries with the British upper classes. For some reason the British have been careful to exclude the University of London from the redbricks, to which it certainly belongs geographically. The term gained currency from the 1940s, perhaps as a result of Bruce Truscot's book *Redbrick University* (1943).

❧ *Red Dog* ❧

There are, of course, canine animals that may be called red. Indeed, Patrick Reginald Chalmers (1872–1942) wrote a poem titled *The Red Dogs*, about various breeds of Irish setter. Nevertheless, over the years this term has had a number of quite disparate meanings.

In the early nineteenth-century United States a *red dog* was an American bank note, and from approximately 1830 to 1860 it was a worthless private bank, much like the wildcat banks, which issued far more notes than it could redeem. Such banks were eliminated by the National Banking Act of 1863, when the name "red dog" for them fell into disuse.

In the 1920s red dog was the name of a card game also known as "high card pool," played with an ordinary deck of cards and poker chips. The players bet in turn that their hands contain a card of the same suit as the top card of the pool (undealt cards) but of higher rank. The reason for the name is not clear.

In the 1950s red dog became an American football play. Originally it was a defensive tactic in which a linebacker shot through the offensive line to tackle the quarterback before he could throw a pass. The linebacker thus "dogged" or "hounded" passes, whence the *dog* of the term. The *red* refers to a code developed by coach Clark Shaughnessy wherein red meant one linebacker, blue meant two linebackers, and green meant three. From this code, only the red survived. (Another writer ascribes the term's origin to New York Giants player Don Ettinger. Normally an offensive guard, this red-headed athlete, whose nickname was "Red," filled in as linebacker in one game and rushed the quarterback. He later explained that he had been "dogging the quarterback a little," hence the expression.)

Another game in which a red dog figures, albeit

loosely, is *red rover*, a children's game popular on both sides of the Atlantic since about 1890. Two parallel lines are drawn about twenty-five feet apart. One player is chosen to be "it" and stands in the center. The others all go behind one of the lines. Then "it" calls out:

> *Red Rover, Red Rover,*
> *Let Rufus come over.*

Rufus, or whichever player's name is called, then tries to get to the other line without being tagged by "it." The game continues from side to side, with "it" calling each player in turn; any player who was tagged stays in the center and helps "it" catch the others. The last player tagged is "it" for the next round of the game.

❧ *Sinful Scarlet* ❧

> *When I am dead, I hope it may be said:*
> *"His sins were scarlet, but his books were read."*
>
> —HILAIRE BELLOC, *Epigrams* (1906)

Scarlet, a brilliant shade of red, became permanently associated with sin through St. John's vision of the *scarlet woman* (also see above). As pointed out, in the biblical account she is thought to have represented pagan Rome, which had the blood of many Christian martyrs on its hands. Much later the term began to be applied to the Church of Rome, mainly by Protestants, and to Protestantism by Catholics. It also was applied to other cities identified with sin, specifically London and Paris, as well as to any woman of loose morals, a prostitute or a sexually promiscuous woman. Undoubtedly this identification is the source of the practice of making a woman convicted of adultery wear a scarlet letter *A* on her clothing, hauntingly described in Nathaniel Hawthorne's novel *The Scarlet Letter* (1850).

Another emblem is responsible for the title and chief character of *The Scarlet Pimpernel*, a popular swashbuckling novel by Baroness Orczy. Pimpernel is the common name of a flower of the primrose family, which the novel's hero adopted as his emblem.

In Shakespeare's day, *dyeing scarlet* meant heavy drinking; he even defined the term in *Henry IV*, Part 1: "They call drinking deep dyeing scarlet" (2:4). This usage is obsolete, as is the figurative meaning of *scarlet fever*, love of the army (or of a man in a uniform). James Grant used this locution in *Romance of War* (1846): "All the young ladies were quite in love with him, touched with the scarlet fever." But this usage left the vocabulary along with the redcoats of the British military.

Unfortunately the medical condition called *scarlet fever* is not yet obsolete, although it has become much less common, at least in the industrialized countries. A contagious disease, it is caused by a streptococcus. Nowadays it is readily prevented from progressing to a serious stage or causing massive epidemics with prompt antibiotic treatment. The disease, also called *scarlatina*, is named for its characteristic manifestations: a pink-red rash, flushed face, bright red tongue, and dark red lines in the creases of skin folds. It has been so called since about 1600.

There are, of course, many other shades of red besides scarlet. They include *vermilion*, very similar to scarlet; *crimson*, a deeper, purplish red; and *garnet*, a dark, deep red like that of the semiprecious stone of that name. None, however, figures very much in idioms and other linguistic associations. A possible exception is crimson, which is strongly identified with Harvard University, at least in Cambridge, Massachusetts.

White as Snow

*W*hite is, strictly speaking, the absence of all color. Or rather, it is the "color" produced by reflecting almost all kinds of light as found in the visible spectrum. It is for this reason that white clothing is cooler than other colors in the hot sun; it reflects back sunlight (and heat) rather than absorbing it, as black does.

The word "white" comes from the Old English *hwit*, which in turn is related to very similar words in various old Germanic languages. It often is defined as the color of snow or milk. Symbolically white has long represented purity, goodness, and innocence. "And I am black, but O! my soul is white," wrote William Blake in his poem *The Little Black Boy* (1789), echoing this sentiment.

More prosaically, white also stands for cleanliness.

In the 1930s and 1940s, the heyday of the American radio soap opera, one well-known sponsor, the maker of Rinso soap powder, thrived on the jingle *Rinso white, Rinso white, happy little washday song!* Some years later, not to be outdone, a manufacturer of detergents claimed that its product would make clothes *Whiter than white*, whatever that might mean.

In heraldry white is called *argent* and similarly stands for purity, truth, and innocence. This word comes from the Latin *argentum*, for silver. Appropriately, "white" has been thieves' slang for "silver" since the seventeenth century (according to Eric Partridge).

🐝 *White as . . .* 🐝

Mary had a little lamb,
Its fleece was white as snow.

> —SARA JOSEPHA HALE,
> *Poems for Our Children* (1830)

The above-quoted nursery rhyme may or may not have been written by Mrs. Hale—her authorship is disputed —but there is no question that it incorporates one of the most common similes involving white. *White as* and *whiter than snow* appeared in English literature as long ago as the year 1000. A popular variant was *white as the driven snow*, which was used by the Latin poet Ovid in his *Metamorphoses*, appeared in English by about 1300, and was common by the sixteenth century. John Lyly wrote, "The fish is white as the driven snow" (*Euphues and his England*, 1579), and Shakespeare had the simile in *The Winter's Tale* (4:3).

White as milk, which along with snow appears in many current dictionary definitions of the color white,

was part of an ancient Greek proverb and appeared in English about 1240 in a translation of the *Roman de la Rose* (possibly made by Chaucer). Chaucer also had *white as chalk*, a common material in England with its *white cliffs of Dover*. "As whyt as chalk" appears in his *The Squire's Tale*.

All of these similes remain current. Another equally old one but heard less often today is *white as a whale's bone*. It, too, dates from the fourteenth century, and Shakespeare had it in *Love's Labour's Lost* (5:2). He also used *white as a sheet*, or rather, *whiter* (in *Cymbeline*, 2:2), which is still often heard. Other early similes include *white as flour*, *white as glass*, and *white as a lily* (and *lily-white*), all from the early 1300s; *white as a swan*, fourteenth century; *white as a kerchief* and *white as ivory*, sixteenth century.

And this list is only partial. One easily could include *white as alabaster*, *a blanched almond*, *an angel*, *ashes*, *a tallow candle*, *bleached cambric*, *a corpse*, *a curd*, *death*, *a ghost*, *a hound's tooth*, *marble*, *a shroud*, *wool*, and probably several dozen others, but most of them are obsolete.

Some of these similes are complimentary and others are far from it. White as marble, alabaster, or a lily often were (and remain) poetic expressions of beauty (but see more about LILY-WHITE below). English poets in particular had a penchant for extolling ladies with skin as white as any of these. Robert Herrick poked fun at them back in the seventeenth century, in a poem published in *Hesperides* (1648):

> *Fain would I kiss my Julia's dainty leg,*
> *Which is as white and hairless as an egg.*

To be *white as a sheet* or *white as death*, on the other hand, usually means to be enraged, terrified, or extremely ill. Writers have described someone being *white with* an emotion such as anger or fear—that is, a face become pale with strong emotion—since at least the fifteenth century. William Caxton, in his translation of *The Foure Sonnes of Aymon* (c. 1489), wrote, "Pale as a white cloth . . . for wrathe." This idea is carried even further with *white-hot*, literally meaning hotter than red-hot and figuratively used since the early nineteenth century for intense emotion, as in "white-hot anger" or "white-hot excitement."

White shrouds, white ghosts, white faces—all these indicate the close associations of white with death. "He lies white-faced and still in the coffin," wrote Walt Whitman (1819–92) in *Reconciliation*. Moreover, *to walk in white* was a metaphor, now largely obsolete, for "to die." Nathaniel P. Willis wrote, "My aunt blessed me shortly before she was called to 'walk in white' " (*Life, Here and There*, 1850).

⚬ *White-haired and Hoary* ⚬

White hair and a *white beard* usually only come with advanced age, and they have often been used as metaphors for the elderly. A *whitebeard* has meant an old man since at least 1450; Shakespeare used the term in *Richard II*: "White-beards have arm'd their thin and hairless scalps against thy majesty" (3:2). But white hair does not always mean that. A sudden shock allegedly can turn hair white (or gray) overnight. Byron alluded to this possibility in *The Prisoner of Chillon* (quoted under OLD AND GRAY).

Yet *white-haired* or *white-headed boy* or *son* have had still another meaning since the sixteenth century: a special favorite or pet. Thomas Fuller used it in his *The History of the Holy Way* (1639): "The pope was loath to adventure his darlings into danger; those white boys were to stay at home with his holiness." Although this idea today is more often conveyed by *fair-haired boy*, it was still used by Eugene O'Neill in *The Great God Brown* (1926): "She gave me the gate. You're the original white-haired boy."

⚬ *Women in White* ⚬

Among the earliest women identified by their white apparel were various orders of nuns known as *White Sisters*, beginning in the twelfth century. The most recently established of these orders is the Congregation of the Missionary Sisters of Our Lady of Africa, founded in 1869, the female counterpart of the WHITE FATHERS (see below). Some orders, among them the Cistercian nuns, were instead called *White Ladies*, but all were so named for their white habits. Today these terms may be retained even though many religious orders have replaced their traditional garb with ordinary street dress.

The *White Lady* also belongs to folklore, where she figured as a ghostly apparition that foretold a death in the house where she appeared. Dr. Ebenezer Brewer believed her ultimate source was the Teutonic myth of Hulda (or Berchta), a goddess dressed in white who received the souls of dead children and young maidens. Another white lady figured in Norman folklore. Appearing outdoors to a wayfarer, she would ask the traveler to dance, and if refused, would throw him in a ditch. Sir Walter Scott's *White Lady of Avenel* is based on these legends.

> *O Lord, sir, when a heroine goes mad she always goes into white satin.*
>
> —RICHARD BRINSLEY SHERIDAN,
> *The Critic* (1779)

By the eighteenth century the traditional apparition of a woman in white was not necessarily a ghost; she could be insane. Sheridan made fun of this convention in his brilliant burlesque of contemporary drama, quoted from above, but Wilkie Collins nevertheless used it to great advantage. His *The Woman in White* (1860), which along with his *The Moonstone* (1868) started a new genre of full-length detective novels, has the title character in just such a role and indeed at the center of the mystery.

On the other hand, the *white witch*, an older term, denotes a witch who practices so-called *white magic*, sorcery where the Devil is not invoked (in contrast to BLACK MAGIC). She is mentioned in Robert Burton's *The Anatomy of Melancholy* (1621) and apparently was still a familiar figure in 1855, when Charles Kingsley wrote: "When he had warts or burns, he went to the white witch at Northam to charm them away" (*Westward Ho!*).

White slavery, although perhaps much older in practice than its name, only began to be called that about the late eighteenth century, when it had a slightly different meaning as well. A congressional debate in 1789 concerned *white slaves* imported from jails in Europe. Presumably it referred not to convict labor but rather to indentured servants who, as a price for their freedom, came to America and had to work for a period of years. No gender was indicated, so the term probably applied to both men and women.

A century later, however, the term was used exclusively for girls and young women who were kidnapped or lured into houses of prostitution, where they were kept captive and forced to work. The name was used to distinguish them from the now outlawed "black slavery" of the southern states. This practice, too, was eventually outlawed. The Mann Act of 1910, popularly called the *White Slave Act*, made it a crime to transport women from one state to another for "immoral" purposes. It did not succeed, however, and interstate trade in prostitutes, which was controlled by organized crime syndicates, continued. Moreover, the law was abused by blackmailers, who used it to entrap men crossing state lines with women quite willing to do so, and in the 1920s it was finally repealed.

🉐 Men in White 🉐

Since the early fifteenth century the Carmelites have been called *White Friars* on account of their white robes. Moreover, the location of their convent in Fleet Street, London, led the district around it to be known as Whitefriars, a name still used.

The *White Fathers* are a French order, the Society of Missionaries of Africa, founded in Algiers in 1868. Their name is a straight translation of the French *Pères Blancs*. In early nineteenth-century America, however, a *white father* denoted a white man who protected and/or controlled persons of another race. This term was not very long-lived but appeared in print in 1835 (according to the *OED*).

Yet another kind of man in white is the *white knight*, who, even though the era of knighthood had long since ended by then, dates only from the late nineteenth century. Presumably this heroic champion was based on the legendary medieval "knight in shining armor" who would come to the rescue of a fair damsel in distress. A parody of this idea, and perhaps also of the *white knight* piece in the game of chess, was personified by Lewis Carroll's white knight in *Through the Looking Glass* (1872). An enthusiastic but impractical inventor of such objects as horse anklets to guard his steed against shark bites, he was dressed in ill-fitting tin armor and kept falling off his horse. This figure of fun gave rise to the metaphoric use of "white knight" for a well-meaning but inefficient or impractical person, but this usage was not long-lived. A new meaning arose in the 1970s, when a company coming to the rescue of a business facing a hostile takeover began to be called a *white knight*. By the 1990s this designation had been broadened to include any sort of financial rescuer. "White Knight Falls Off His Charger," proclaimed the *New York Times* headline (May 16, 1991) of an article describing the failure of financier Felix G. Rohatyn to bail out New York City from its financial quagmire.

> *She was awfully old for a white wedding, thirty or something terrible.*
>
> —NANCY MITFORD,
> *Love in a Cold Climate* (1949)

White apparel is not, of course, confined to knights in armor or religious orders. For centuries brides have been wearing a white gown and veil, symbolizing purity and virginity, and when they do, the ceremony is said to be a *white wedding*.

On particularly elegant occasions a man may be asked to come in *white tie* and "tails"—that is, formal dress with a white bow tie and swallowtail coat. This attire has been around since the mid-nineteenth century. "I suppose you would go properly dressed—white tie, kids, and that sort of thing, eh?" wrote E. Bradley (*The Adventures of Mr. Verdant Green*, 1853).

White gloves also were an article of formal dress. Since touching anything while wearing white gloves risks soiling them, they came to symbolize anything immaculate or sterile, as well as meticulous and painstaking. A *white-glove inspection*—literally running a white-gloved hand over surfaces to make sure they are absolutely clean—now is used figuratively for a very careful inspection, and *white-glove treatment* similarly refers to painstaking treatment.

Wearing a *white coat* over street clothes when seeing patients has been customary for physicians, ambulance attendants, and other medical practitioners since the early twentieth century. About midcentury came the expression *Here come the little men in white coats*, whereby the speaker implied, usually in jest, that the person being addressed was crazy and would be carted off to an asylum by white-coated attendants.

By the early 1920s, work attire that included a *white collar* on a shirt had become a synonym for office work, sales, and similar kinds of employment (as opposed to manual labor) and for those engaged in such work. It was spelled out by Upton Sinclair in *The Brass Check* (1919), writing about union men as opposed to clerks, "who are allowed to wear a white collar." A 1921 issue of the *Ladies' Home Journal* had, "Urban chain restaurants have accustomed white-collar boys and girls to tasty viands" (cited by the *OED*).

By the mid-twentieth century white collars had a darker side. The term *white-collar crime* was probably coined by Edwin H. Sutherland, who used it as the title of his 1949 book about business and professional persons breaking the law in the course of pursuing their occupations. Embezzling, tax evasion, fraud, and the theft of office equipment all fell into this newly named category.

During the same period, the 1940s and 1950s, a style of white leather shoe became the collegiate rage. It was called *white bucks* (short for "buckskin"), and wearing them indicated that one belonged to the high-fashion "in" group on campus.

Wearing a *white belt*, on the other hand, means that one is a rank beginner in judo, karate, and related martial arts. Slightly advanced expertise may allow one to wear a yellow belt, but only the highest skill entitles one to a BLACK BELT.

⮆ *The Great Whitewash* ⮆

*Like it? Well, I don't see why I oughtn't to like it.
Does a boy get a chance to whitewash a fence every
day?*

—MARK TWAIN, *Tom Sawyer* (1875)

Tom's brilliant discovery that making a hated chore seem highly desirable will persuade others to do the work, and even pay for the privilege, is one of the early high points of this novel.

The noun *whitewash* for a liquid compound of lime and water or some similar substance for whitening walls, ceilings, and the like has been around since the late seventeenth century, and the verb form, for whitening walls, is a hundred years older still. By the mid-eighteenth century *to whitewash* also was being used figuratively as meaning to conceal faults, exonerate from blame, or generally make something ugly appear to be beautiful. Thus Horace Walpole wrote: "A poet and an author will go as far in whitewashing a munificent tyrant" (*Memoirs of the Reign of George the Third*, 1764).

In America during this same period, to whitewash also meant to clear an insolvent from liability. By simply declaring oneself bankrupt, one could discharge oneself from one's debts. *The Boston Evening Post* of August 2, 1762, said: "Another [man], lately white-washed (taken the benefit of the Bankrupt Act), proposed to me my setting him up again in business" (quoted in Richard H. Thornton's *American Glossary*, 1912). This meaning for whitewash is now obsolete, but another, acquired at about the same time, is still current: a sports or game victory so complete that the loser fails to score at all.

The most common figurative use of whitewash, however, is still that of a cover-up. President Richard Nixon so used it in a speech in April 1973, denying any concealment in the Watergate scandal: "There will be no whitewash in the White House."

The figurative use of white, or good, to conceal black, or evil, is very old indeed. In the Gospel of St. Matthew, Jesus preaches, "Woe unto you, scribes and Pharisees, hypocrites! for ye are like unto whited sepulchers, which indeed appear beautiful outward but are within full of dead men's bones, and of all uncleanness" (Matthew 23:27). Jesus was alluding to the ancient custom of whitening a tomb (*whited sepulcher*) to make it conspicuous, so that passersby could not accidentally defile it. Even though both "whited" and "sepulcher" now sound archaic, the term continues to be used for hypocrisy—that is, concealing wickedness under a cloak of virtue.

Much as *white magic* is, relative to black magic, "good" magic, a *white list* is the counterpart of a BLACKLIST. Whereas the blacklist condemns, the white list approves. A term used since about 1900, it denotes a catalog of "acceptable" people or things: employers who meet union standards for working conditions; businesses approved for patronage because of their affiliations, practices, or policies; films and books approved for youngsters; etc.

Similarly evoking the notion that white stands for morally pure and free from evil intent is the term *white lie*, used since the eighteenth century for a venial falsehood or harmless fib. Often a white lie is uttered out of sheer politeness—for example, (A): "Do you like my new coat?" (B): "Yes, it's lovely"—when B privately thinks the coat is hideous. Margot Asquith (1865–1945), known for her acerbic wit, once said of a friend, "She tells enough white lies to ice a wedding cake." *Little White Lies* (1930), by Walter Donaldson, was a hit song in its time, popularized first by bandleader Guy Lombardo and later by Frank Sinatra.

Well—this is white of you.

—EDITH WHARTON,
The Custom of the Country (1913)

The slangy expression *That's white of you* has been around since at least 1875. Originally American, it quickly crossed the Atlantic. "White" here means honorable, fair, and/or decent. Eric Partridge believed it originated in the American South. If that is the case, it probably contains an implicit racist bias, which should curtail its use today. However, he offered no verification for this origin, and if, like "white lie," the term alludes to moral decency, there is no reason not to use it.

❧ *The White Man's Burden* ❧

The use of *white* for *white race* appears to date only from the seventeenth century; the *OED*'s earliest citation is from 1695. From the point of view of color, of course, it is as much a misnomer as *black* is for the brown-skinned; few if any human beings, even those with pigment deficiencies known as *albino*, have pure-white skin. Nevertheless, the term won wide acceptance and remains current.

The differentiation of races by color has traditionally favored the white. Much as white is symbolically equated with good and black with evil, white men (and women) long tended to regard themselves as superior to those of darker skin color. Linguistically this view has taken the form of such terms (and policies) as *white supremacy*, originating in the United States immediately following the Civil War. White supremacists insist that their race is superior to all others, especially the black, and they

thus are entitled to rule over all. The term became particularly prominent in the mid-1960s under Prime Minister Ian Smith and his attempts, unsuccessful in the end,
to retain the white minority's rule over the black majority
of Southern Rhodesia (now the Republic of Zimbabwe).
Both the term and the concept survive in present-day
America.

Smith's views had roots in the nineteenth century,
when British imperialist policies declared it was *the white
man's burden* or duty to govern and educate less civilized,
"backward" nonwhites. Rudyard Kipling's 1899 poem
The White Man's Burden gave this term wide currency:

> *Take up the White Man's Burden—*
> *Send forth the best you breed,*
> *Go bind your sons to exile*
> *To serve the captives' need.*

Today, of course, this view is widely regarded as incred-
ibly self-serving and smug.

Colonizing was not without its hazards. In 1836
F. H. Rankin wrote a book about Sierra Leone entitled
The White Man's Grave. This term was taken up as an
apt description for much of West Africa, whose unhealthy
(for Europeans) climate and tropical diseases claimed
many colonists' lives (as the tropics did in other parts of
the world).

Another term born in Africa, but dating only from
the twentieth century, is *white hunter* for a white man
who engages in guiding others on safaris, in search of big
game. Although it can be (and is) used for any white man
who hunts, the term is generally confined to the professional hunter. Nancy Mitford used it in *The Pursuit of
Love* (1945): "She's happy now, isn't she, with her white
hunter?"

Even during the early nineteenth century, white in
the sense of race did not always betoken superior. *Poor*

whites and *white trash* were a class regarded with contempt in the American South by both blacks and whites. "The slave of a gentleman universally considers himself a superior being to 'poor white folks,'" according to a Virginian gentleman's letter printed in J. K. Paulding's *Slavery in the United States* (1836), and an 1833 entry in Fanny Kemble's *Journal* said that slaves referred to white servants as *poor white trash*. These terms are still used, along with *whitey*, a contemptuous term often employed by blacks during the 1960s civil rights struggles.

A more positive concept is denoted in *white hope*. This term was originally coined to signify a white boxer who might defeat Jack Johnson, the first black heavyweight champion. Johnson was seemingly invincible, holding the title from 1908 until he was finally defeated by Jess Willard in 1915 in Havana, Cuba. By 1919 or so, *white hope* had been extended to signify any individual or object of whom great achievement is anticipated, or at least hoped.

White as a lily, and its companion, *lily-white*, have been used since the fourteenth century to mean beautiful and pure. At the turn of the twentieth century in the United States, however, they were used to describe racially segregated groups or facilities. In the course of the civil rights movement of the 1960s this meaning was abandoned, or fell into disfavor along with segregation. However, "lily-white" continued to be used to mean "perfect," which covered every respect, including honesty. Thus "a lily-white police force" no longer meant one that was confined to white officers but rather one composed of incorruptible officers, who could not be bribed.

The civil rights movement also embraced the ideal of human brotherhood, whereby the black man should be regarded and treated as the *white man's brother*, a term that gained some currency. In this context, Martin Luther King, Jr., said in a 1962 speech, "I want to be the white man's brother, not his brother-in-law" (quoted in the *New York Journal-American*).

Despite efforts to eliminate it, at least in areas where it amounts to discrimination, black and white differentiation continues in American culture. In the 1970s linguists coined the term *white English* for the speech patterns and vocabulary that predominate among white Americans. Its counterpart, *black English*, had been identified several decades earlier. In Canada *Speak white* is, according to linguist Mario Pei (*The Story of Language*, 1965), the English-speaking Canadian's put-down to French Canadians, alluding both to their accent and their mixed (with Indian) blood.

🥨 *Craven and Cowardly White* 🥨

In view of its many positive connotations, it seems strange that white should also be associated with fear and cowardice, but it is. *White-livered* has meant cowardly since the mid-sixteenth century, a usage stemming from the popular belief that a light-colored liver was deficient in bile, or "choler," and consequently deficient in spirit and courage. John Heywood's proverb collection of 1546 included this strange mixed metaphor: "Thinke ye me so whyte lyuerd [livered] (quoth shee) that I wyll be toung-tyed?" The use of "white-livered" has not survived, but its contemporary, *lily-livered*, with precisely the same meaning (and origin, since it refers to white lilies), is still current.

One need not look inside the body to observe human fear; it is readily seen in a *white face* and in the *white knuckles* of a hand clenched with apprehension. The observation is surely older, but the latter term, and adjectival use of it describing a cause for such fear—for example, an airplane's *white-knuckle* approach to a fogged-in airport—dates only from the twentieth century.

To *bleed someone white* has meant to extort money, or take someone's last penny, since the seventeenth century. One writer hypothesizes that it was coined by gamblers. Once their victim had been made to pay through the nose—that is, lost all his blood through his nose—he was bled white. More likely, however, the saying alludes to the fact that money was considered the lifeblood of trade and commerce. Raymond Chandler, a writer well acquainted with the language of criminals, used the expression in a discussion of writing: "It is the writers' own weakness as craftsmen that permits the superior egos to bleed them white of initiative, imagination, and integrity" (*Raymond Chandler Speaks*, 1945).

❧ White Feathers and Flags ❧

To *show the white feather* also meant a display of cowardice, at least in England (some American Indians regarded it as a peace signal). This usage dates from the late eighteenth century and comes from cockfighting. The pure gamecock has no white tail feathers; their presence would indicate that he is of degenerate stock. The term was transferred to signify human cowardice by 1785, when Grose so defined it in his compendium of slang.

Oddly enough, at this same time a *white cockade* had no such meaning. In 1784 Johnson's dictionary had, "Boswell, in the year 1745 . . . wore a white cockade, and prayed for King James." Both the white cockade in this period and the *white flag* from the seventeenth century on were associated with royalist causes. In France the white flag was that of the Bourbon kings, used until they were overthrown in the French Revolution. Simultaneously, however, and dating back even further, *showing a white flag* meant either surrender in battle or a willingness to negotiate a truce. Philemon Holland's 1600 translation of the Roman historian Livy's writings mentions a Carthaginian warship bearing a white flag in token of suspending hostilities to parley. And today the white flag remains an international symbol of surrender or truce.

&a& *The Whites of Their Eyes* &a&

Among the most famous orders that come to us from the American Revolution is, "Men, you are all marksmen— don't one of you fire until you see the whites of their eyes." Allegedly the colonists received this order from General Israel Putnam or Colonel William Prescott, or even some other officer, on June 17, 1775, at the Battle of Bunker Hill (then called Breed's Hill), won by the British. The key portion of the order, which of course meant to hold fire until one was sure of hitting the target, eventually became a general catchphrase on both sides of the Atlantic. Today we still say *don't fire until you see the whites of their eyes* in any kind of situation where we are warning someone against acting prematurely.

The white portions of the eyeballs, incidentally, have been so called since about 1400. From about 1480 on, to *turn up the whites of the eyes* meant to make a great show of devotion, as well as to show astonishment, horror, or some similar strong emotion. Thus Tobias Smollett wrote,

"Mrs. Tabitha . . . threw up the whites of her eyes as if in the act of ejaculation" (*Humphry Clinker*, 1771). This expression, however, appears to be obsolescent, at least in America.

White Elephant for Sale

In Buddhism, the white or albino elephant is the form in which Gautama came to his mother, white symbolizing the divine and the elephant symbolizing wisdom.

Many American Indian tribes showed enormous respect for albino animals. They were thought to have supernatural powers and so were feared as well as sought after. Some tribes regarded seeing an albino as bad luck. The Seneca used white dogs for sacrifices, and the Plains tribes used white buffalo.

In Siam (Thailand), according to legend, only the king was permitted to own an albino elephant, and consequently these animals were considered sacred. No one might ride one or kill one without special permission from the king. Like the pigmented members of their species, however, albino elephants have an appetite proportionate to their size and hence are expensive to feed. According to legend, when the king was displeased with one of his courtiers, he would present him with a white elephant and calmly wait until the costs of keeping it caused the owner to be ruined.

Whether or not this custom actually existed is not known, but it was believed widely enough so that the term *white elephant* acquired its present-day meaning, an unwanted possession that is hard to get rid of but too valuable to throw out or abandon. It is a standby of church bazaars and garage sales, which count on such objects as Aunt Matilda's hideous pink glass bowl with real ivory and silver handles to be admired enough to bring in revenue.

In contrast, a *white sale* is a special offering, usually at reduced prices, of *white goods*—towels, bed and table linens, and related wares. The term originated in America around the turn of the twentieth century; a 1900 store catalog announces a white sale. Since about 1960, however, the term "white goods" also has been used for home appliances that are traditionally made with white cases —refrigerators, washing machines, and clothes dryers.

A *white market*, on the other hand, has nothing to do with these products, at least not necessarily. This term, originating in the late 1940s, describes the legal buying and selling of ration coupons, whose price is determined by the demand and supply of the rationed commodities. Such a practice is allowed in order to prevent a BLACK MARKET in these items. In the mid-1970s, following OPEC's fourfold increase in world oil prices, some American officials proposed a system of gasoline rationing and the creation of a white market for gas coupons.

❧ *White Spirits* ❧

The oldest of so-called white alcoholic beverages, which is no more "white" than a white person's skin, is *white wine*. This name has been used since the fourteenth century for any light-colored, transparent wine; John Langland refers to it in *Piers Ploughman* (1377). Traditionally, white table wines accompany fish or *white meat*, as the flesh of veal, chicken, and pork have been called since the eighteenth century.

White table wine ranges from 9 to 12 percent or so in alcohol content. A much stronger drink is *white mule*, a liquor distilled from corn and so called for its clear color and, Partridge suggests, the strength of a mule's kick. It is closely related (or even identical) to *white lightning*, similarly named for its color and effect. Both are names for moonshine—illegally distilled whiskey—and originated in the American South. They are green whiskeys fresh from the still, which might consist of a copper wash boiler, a length of pipe, an old shotgun barrel, and a cotton blanket. If allowed to age, the whiskeys might turn into a smooth bourbon; as it is, they are quite raw.

More genteel by far is the *white lady*, a cocktail devised in the late 1920s. It consists of lemon juice, Cointreau, egg whites, and gin, combined and shaken with cracked ice. In Australia, however, this same name means methylated spirits (denatured alcohol), which can have a dire effect when consumed.

❧ *Dreaming of a White Christmas* ❧

The term *white Christmas* today is firmly associated with Irving Berlin's nostalgic 1942 song of that name. Berlin did not originate the term, and certainly not the idea of a snowy holiday season. Charles Kingsley had it in *Two Years Ago* (1857): "We shall have a white Christmas, I expect."

Snow is all very well, but a *whiteout* can be too much of a good thing. At first meteorologists used the term for a condition found only in arctic regions when snow-covered ground and cloud-covered sky combine to make other features of the landscape, such as the horizon, indistinguishable. In the 1940s, however, the word began to be used more generally for any heavy blizzard or snowstorm in which visibility became very limited. And in the 1970s the word, in a somewhat altered form as a trademark, Wite-Out, acquired still another meaning: white correction fluid used to obscure errors in typing or artwork.

> *God makes sech nights, all white an' still,*
> *Fur'z you can look or listen,*
> *Moonshine and snow on field an' hill.*

> —JAMES RUSSELL LOWELL,
> *Biglow Papers* (1867)

In the high latitudes of the earth, on the night of the summer solstice, it never gets completely dark. One can walk outdoors at one or two o'clock in the morning and see well enough to read without artificial light. About the middle of the twentieth century this condition began to be called *white night*, a term that had been used earlier for a sleepless night. The latter usage comes from the French idiom *passer une nuit blanc*, which was used in English since about 1900 but which is currently obsolete.

Another strange weather phenomenon is the *white squall*, which occurs at sea. It consists of a violent localized disturbance involving high waves and turbulent waters but not accompanied by dark clouds and diminished light. This term has been used since about 1800.

> *But seas do laugh, show white, when rocks are*
> *near.*

> —JOHN WEBSTER, *The White Devil* (c. 1608)

A crested wave or breaker has been called a *whitecap* since the late seventeenth century. (The same name has been used for species of birds and mushrooms as well.) Poets have referred to whitecaps as *white horses*; for example, Matthew Arnold in his *The Forsaken Merman* (1849):

> *Now the wild white horses play,*
> *Champ and chafe and toss in the spray.*

Also, shallow or shoal waters, with breakers or foam, have been called *white water* since the sixteenth century, but the sport of *whitewater rafting* has been so called only since about 1900.

❧ *From Whitehall to White House* ❧

The sentinel on Whitehall gate looked forth into the night.

—THOMAS MACAULAY, *The Armada* (1848)

One of London's grandest palaces was built in the thirteenth century, in the reign of Henry III. It was called York Place, and its last occupant under that name was one of England's most famous churchmen, Cardinal Wolsey. After dismissing Wolsey for treason in 1530, Henry VIII took over the palace and renamed it. Shakespeare relates this event in *Henry VIII* (4:1): "Sir, you must no more call it York-place; that's past; for, since the cardinal fell, that title's lost: 'tis now the king's, and call'd Whitehall." The palace was used until 1698, when a fire destroyed nearly all of it. Only the great banquet hall, designed by Inigo Jones, survived. However, the name was passed on to the London street where it stood and where many government offices were located. Consequently, Whitehall came to mean government offices in general, and by extension, the British civil service.

Another hallmark of British government is the *white paper*, a name used since the seventeenth century for a government publication printed for the information of Parliament. It may consist of a report, policy statement, or some other document that is not lengthy enough to required being bound as a blue book (see also BLUE BOOKS).

The American symbol for and residence of the nation's chief executive, the *White House*, is much newer, although it is the oldest public building in Washington, D.C. Its cornerstone was laid by George Washington in 1792, and John Adams was the first president to reside there. In 1814 the building was burned by British troops,

but it was restored and the smoke-stained gray stone was painted white. It had been called the White House even prior to this paint job, but the name became official only much later, when President Theodore Roosevelt had it engraved on his stationery. Although it contains some government offices, the name White House is loosely used for anyone or anything connected to the executive branch, regardless of housing. The media thus refer to "White House spokesmen," "White House staff," "White House directives," and so on, without regard to their physical location or source.

New York City boasts no comparable public buildings but does have *the Great White Way*, as Broadway from Fifty-ninth Street to Times Square has been called since about 1900. The title of a 1901 novel by Albert Bigelow Paine, an American writer known primarily for children's stories and biographies, the term refers to the bright lights, both literal and figurative, of the city's theater district. By 1920 the term was being transferred to brightly lit thoroughfares of other cities (by Sinclair Lewis in his novel *Main Street*, for one), but this usage did not persist for long, and the term has remained identified with New York.

White Russians

Since the early twentieth century, Russian counter-revolutionaries, the opponents of first the Bolsheviks and later the Communists, have been known as *White Russians*. The Whites represented all shades of anti-Communist groups. Some were in favor of setting up a military dictatorship, and a few were outspoken royalists. Nevertheless, they fought bitterly against the Reds (Communists), a civil war that lasted until the Whites were finally defeated in 1920.

However, there is another kind of White Russian— a *Belorussian*, a native of Belorussia, or White Russia, which became one of the republics making up the Union of Soviet Socialist Republics. The source of its name is disputed. Some linguists believe it reflects the fact that the western Russians were called "white" by the Muscovite Russians. Others hold that the name really means "free," as opposed to Tatar-controlled (eastern) Russia. Still others believe it alludes to the fair hair and white native costumes of the population. Still another theory is based on the fact that in some languages colors are associated with directions; according to this line of thought, white was long associated with west, and Belorussia is so named because it is the westernmost part of Russia.

Yellow Jack

*Y*ellow, the color of gold, but-
ter, lemons, egg yolks, and sunlight, lies between green
and orange on the spectrum and is, along with red and
blue, one of the primary colors. The word *yellow* has been
part of the English language since about A.D. 900, coming
from closely related words in Latin and various Germanic
languages.

In heraldry, where it is called *or* (for gold), yellow
stands for the positive virtues of faith, constancy, wisdom,
and glory. In thieves' slang it also frequently describes
something desirable—gold or something made of gold.

The simile *yellow as gold* is among the oldest still in
use. Chaucer had it in *The Knight's Tale*: "Yelowe and
brighte as any gold." In the prologue to *The Canterbury
Tales* he also had *yellow as wax* ("This pardoner had heer

as yelow as wex"), which is obsolete. Other early comparisons are *yellow as a kite's foot* and *yellow as a marigold*, both dating from the early seventeenth century. Izaak Walton used the latter in *The Compleat Angler* (1653), but it is not heard much today. A later simile, *yellow as a guinea*, meaning the gold coin, was especially common during the nineteenth century but has died out along with the coin. The coin itself was called a *yellow boy* for a time, both in Britain and the United States.

In most other contexts, however, yellow, like black, has many negative associations. Among them are jealousy, treachery, cowardice, aging, illness, and various races regarded as threatening or inferior. We also have ambivalence concerning the attractiveness of yellow. *Yellow hair*, for example, is fine if by it we mean blond or golden hair; if the white hair of old age acquires a yellowish tinge, we tend to consider it ugly. The *yellow skin* of jaundice or old age (see below) is far from beautiful, nor do we admire yellowish teeth, which toothpaste manufacturers urge us to whiten by using their product. "*You'll wonder where the yellow went* when you brush your teeth with Pepsodent" was one of the most successful commercial jingles of the 1950s.

❧ *Jealousy and Treachery* ❧

Blue is true, Yellow's jealous.

—J. O. HALLIWELL,
Nursery Rhymes of England (1842)

The color yellow has symbolized jealousy since Elizabethan times. *He wears yellow stockings* was, from the late sixteenth century through the eighteenth century, a way of saying "He is jealous." Shakespeare referred to it in *Twelfth Night* (2:4): "He will come to her in yellow stockings, and 'tis a colour she abhors." The source of this association has been forgotten, and the usage is now obsolete.

The connection of yellow with treachery is biblical. Judas Iscariot, who betrayed Jesus, is generally portrayed in yellow garb. However, painters also often used yellow clothing for St. Peter, casting some doubts on this association. Nevertheless, during the Spanish Inquisition, those condemned for heresy were dressed in yellow. In France the doors of traitors were marked with yellow paint. In Venice wearing a *yellow hat* was the ancient mark of a Jew, and in other lands at various times Jews wore yellow, as a mark of their historic betrayal of Jesus.

The most blatant such labeling in recent times came during the Nazi era, when Jews were required to wear a *yellow Star of David*. I. Cohen described it (*Jews in War*, 1942):

> *The crowning device for humiliating Jews was the revival of a medieval practice. In October 1941 a decree was issued requiring them to wear a yellow armlet marked with the "shield of David," which the Jews of Poland had been wearing for the past two years.*

Thanks to Hitler, a yellow Star of David will forever be associated with the World War II holocaust.

❧ Sad and Old ❧

My days are in the yellow leaf;
The flowers and fruits of love are gone.

—GEORGE GORDON, LORD BYRON,
On This Day I Complete
My Thirty-Sixth Year (1824)

Shakespeare had Viola speak of her "green and yellow melancholy" (*Twelfth Night*, 2:4) when she describes her grief over secret, unrequited love. He also has Macbeth say: "I have lived long enough: my way of life is fall'n into the sere, the yellow leaf" (*Macbeth*, 5:3).

Probably because green leaves turn yellow in autumn, before dying altogether, yellow became a symbol of desiccation and old age. We speak of the pages of a book *yellowed with age* (both white paper and white fabric do turn color). And Shakespeare graphically described human aging: "Have you not a moist eye, a dry hand, a yellow cheek, a white beard, a decreasing leg, an increasing belly?" (*Henry IV*, Part 2, 1:2).

❧ *A Yellow Streak* ❧

I found the streak of yellow in him.

—GEORGE ADE, *Artie* (1896)

To *be yellow* or to *have a yellow streak* does not necessarily betoken the wear and tear of passing years. Rather, it means cowardice. Although it seems much older, the use of "yellow" for craven and cowardly dates only from the mid-nineteenth century. Originally American, it first appeared in print in a book by P. T. Barnum (of circus fame) in 1856 and rapidly spread to every part of the English-speaking world.

An embroidered version of this expression is *yellow-bellied*, which likewise means cowardly. This term also has a quite literal meaning when applied to various animals—for example, the *yellow-bellied sapsucker*, a North American woodpecker, actually has a pale yellow abdomen. The same is true of certain species of eel, and in eighteenth-century England *yellowbelly* was a slang word for people born in the fens of Lincoln, Norfolk, and other counties, likening them to the eels found and consumed there. Later the term, never in a flattering sense, was applied to various ethnic groups: Mexicans, Orientals, Eurasians. Today, however, it tends to be applied mainly to human cowards regardless of race or origin, a usage dating from the early twentieth century.

🙠 *The Jaundiced Eye* 🙠

All looks yellow to the jaundiced eye.

—ALEXANDER POPE,
Essay on Criticism (1711)

Pope's "jaundiced eye" referred to the prejudices of critics that lead them to condemn perfectly good work. But *jaundice* is, of course, a symptom of liver disease that is characterized by a yellow discoloration of the patient's skin and the whites of the eyes (its very name comes from the French word for yellow, *jaune*).

Jaundice is one of the symptoms of *yellow fever*, a severe infectious disease endemic to central Africa and parts of South and Central America. The name was first used for this disorder in the eighteenth century; it appeared in a 1748 medical text that described it as an American name for what was also called the *yellow sickness*.

By the early nineteenth century yellow fever had been encountered by more and more European and American visitors to the tropics and had acquired a nickname, *yellow jack*. Frederick Marryat alluded to it in his *Peter Simple* (1833): "With regard to Yellow Jack, as we calls the Yellow fever, it's a devil incarnate." A highly contagious disease, it is caused by a virus and transmitted by various species of mosquito. The disease claimed many lives until its cause was discovered by an Army surgeon, Walter Reed (1851–1902), who helped institute vigorous mosquito eradication programs in Cuba and the Panama Canal Zone (where American troops were stationed) as a preventive measure. American playwright Sidney Howard told Reed's story in his play *Yellow Jack* (1934). Since then, an effective preventive vaccine has been developed.

In 1825 a law was passed requiring ships to fly a *yellow flag* indicating the presence or absence of contagious disease aboard; this flag also was called a *yellow jack*. A plain yellow flag indicated a clean bill of health; a yellow ground with a black ball in the center indicated disease; and a flag divided into black and yellow quarters indicated a highly contagious disease. In 1931 the new International Code of Signals changed the rules somewhat, but a plain yellow flag still indicates good health; if flown with another flag, it indicates the possibility or presence of disease on board.

In Australia in the nineteenth century *yellow fever* became a colloquialism for gold-prospecting mania. In the United States, on the other hand, *yellow flu* is a neologism of the 1970s. It refers to student absenteeism as a protest against compulsory busing (instituted to desegregate school districts). In effect, students protested by staying home, claiming to be ill with flu. The yellow in the term refers to the standard color of American school buses.

❧ The Yellow Peril ❧

Yellow has been used to describe the skin color of Oriental peoples since the late eighteenth century. In America it was used also to describe those of mixed black and white ancestry—that is, mulattoes; often they were characterized as *yaller*, or *high yaller*, the latter meaning quite light in color. This usage is obsolescent or obsolete.

The first usage of yellow, for Orientals, is now considered demeaning and insulting. Nevertheless, it survives, particularly in such xenophobic terms as *the yellow peril*. This expression originated as a translation of the German *die gelbe Gefahr*, a term of the 1890s referring to the possibility that the densely populated Asian nations would overrun Europe and the rest of the world, winning ultimate control. A New York *Daily News* article of 1900 about threats to trade pointed out that this was "The 'yellow peril' in its most dangerous form." The term is still alive and well. Australian novelist Colleen McCullough used it in *The Thorn Birds* (1977): "But Japan was Asia, part of the Yellow Peril." In recent decades both Australia and New Zealand have seen a large influx of Japanese tourists and investors, and U.S. industry feels its well-being threatened by Japan in such areas as automobile and computer manufacture. While we may consider the term "yellow peril" a hysterical overstatement, the fears it reflects are not dead.

The color yellow is associated with the Orient in less emotional ways as well. The *Yellow Emperor* was Huang Ti, the legendary first emperor of China. The *Yellow Sea*—Hwang Hai in transliterated Chinese—is the portion of the Pacific Ocean that lies between China and Korea. One of China's most important waterways is the *Yellow River*, or Hwang-Ho, which flows 2,800 miles from western China to the Gulf of Bohai. Legend calls it China's celestial river, which rains from heaven to earth as a shower of gold—that is, the sun's rays. A more prosaic explanation for its name is that its waters carry huge amounts of yellow silt.

The *yellowfin tuna* is a species that inhabits the warm waters of both the Atlantic and Pacific oceans. So called from the 1920s, it has become especially valuable

in recent decades because its flesh is particularly prized
for sushi and sashimi, Japanese dishes of raw fish enjoyed
not only in Japan but also increasingly in the West.

Finally, *yellowfish* is an epithet sometimes used for
illegal Chinese immigrants (much as wetbacks is used
for Mexicans). It is, of course, derogatory and offensive.

~ *Yellow Rain* ~

Environmentalists concerned with the effects of war in
Southeast Asia might be surprised to learn that Henry
David Thoreau described *yellow rain* when he lived on
Walden Pond. "The sulphur-like pollen of the pitch pine
soon covered the pond," he wrote (*Walden*, 1854), and he
certainly was not the first to observe this natural phenomenon. The name "yellow rain" for abundant coverage
with pollen appeared in the *Century Dictionary* (1891); it
had earlier been described as *sulphur rain*, that chemical
being yellow in color.

In the 1970s, however, in Cambodia, Laos, and other
Southeast Asian countries, the widespread presence of
powdery yellow deposits on vegetation gave rise to concern, particularly since they contained a harmful toxic
substance. Some analysts claimed it was the product of
chemical warfare being carried on by one or another of
the warring political factions in that part of the world.
Others, however, believed it to be bee excrement that had
somehow become contaminated with a toxic fungus.

If the latter hypothesis is true, conceivably yellow
rain could be caused by *yellow jackets*, an American name
used for wasps and hornets since the mid-nineteenth century. William Dean Howells used it in *The Landlord at
Lion's Head* (1897): "He remembered stumbling into a
nest of yellowjackets."

✺ *Yellow Dog* ✺

The name *yellow dog* originally designated any kind of mongrel dog, and by extension came to mean a worthless creature, a cowardly, ill-bred individual. The term was so used in the United States during the nineteenth century, as it had been in Britain for some time. In the late nineteenth century, as the American labor movement grew in strength, the name was used also for any individual or organization opposed to trade unions. From this usage came the term *yellow-dog contract*, for an agreement that an employee would not join a labor union. Employers used such agreements to fight labor unions, forcing workers to sign a yellow-dog contract as a condition of being hired. The Norris-LaGuardia Act of 1932, however, made yellow-dog contracts unenforceable.

✺ *Yellow in Print* ✺

Yellow journalism, for sensationalist, unscrupulous newspaper coverage, comes from a fierce newspaper rivalry of the 1890s. One of New York's great newspapers during this era was the *World*, which Joseph Pulitzer had bought from financier Jay Gould in 1883. At the time of this purchase it was a two-cent newspaper with a circulation of 15,000. Within two years circulation had been increased to a hitherto unheard-of 230,000. Pulitzer had already built up one great newspaper, the *St. Louis Post-Dispatch*. When he invaded the field in New York, it was with new and radical ideas. The paper soon became known for uncovering scandals, both personal and political, and serving them up to an avid public in luridly illustrated stories bearing screaming headlines. When news was scarce, Pulitzer made news. He sent Nelly Bly around the world by every possible means of transport, from ricksha to airplane, and watched circulation soar with every story of her adventures. The *World* conducted contests and surveys and public-opinion polls. It ran a fund-raising campaign to build a pedestal for the Statue of Liberty in New York Harbor, collecting $100,000 in nickels and dimes from 120,000 individual contributors.

The *World* also reported the important news of the day and developed into a powerful social and political force in the life of New York. The paper's political cartoonists drew so skillful a series during the presidential election campaign of 1884 that the paper was given considerable credit for the victory of Grover Cleveland over James G. Blaine.

In 1895 William Randolph Hearst, who had patterned his *San Francisco Examiner* after Pulitzer's *World*, bought the *New York Morning Journal* and began a bitter circulation fight with Pulitzer. The two papers outdid one another in sensationalism. Hearst raided the staffs of other papers, including the *World*, luring top newsmen with fabulous salaries.

One of Pulitzer's most successful innovations was running regular comic cartoons, especially one drawn by Richard Felton Outcault that made its first appearance in the *Sunday World* of February 16, 1896. It was entitled "The Great Dog Show in McGoogan's Avenue" and depicted a typical backyard in a slum, peopled by street urchins and dogs. Dominating this scene was the *Yellow Kid*, a strange figure of a boy with a wary, somehow old-looking face and clad in a bright yellow nightshirt. The cartoon caught the public imagination, and Pulitzer made it a standard feature of the Sunday color supplement.

As their circulation war reached new heights, Hearst bought numerous *World* staff members away from his rival, among them Outcault. Pulitzer raised the bid and got his men back, but Hearst outbid him again and persuaded Outcault to work for him. Starting on October 16, *Journal* readers were greeted by the Yellow Kid in a new color supplement. Pulitzer countered by hiring a well-known painter, George Luks, to carry on "The Yellow Kid" in the *World*, and for some time the twin cartoons ran in both newspapers.

The pace of the competition became more and more frantic. Almost any story was printed if it promised to lure readers. If murder, scandal, and horrors were in short supply, false stories were invented or trivial events were distorted. Photographs were altered, prominent persons misquoted, and circulation soared.

These practices are what were called *yellow journalism*, named for the Yellow Kid. Historians now believe they were not merely irresponsible, but also helped involve the United States in a war that no one originally wanted. In February 1898 the U.S. battleship *Maine*, which was in Havana (Cuba) Bay at the request of the American consul, blew up, killing 260 Americans aboard. The reason for the explosion was never determined, but the *yellow press* of New York had no trouble inventing its own. Headlines blared over this "outrage," and even though neither the American government nor Spain (which governed Cuba) wanted war, the temper of the American public was so inflamed by the newspaper stories that war became inevitable.

During this same era the reading public on both sides of the Atlantic also had the *yellowback*, ancestor of today's inexpensive paperback. These were cheap reprints of trashy books and magazines, especially French novels, and were so called for their yellow board binding. In England they were sold in railroad bookstalls, and in America at newsstands. They were not to be confused with *The Yellow Book*, a quarterly magazine published from 1894 to 1897 in Britain by John Lane. Its title was chosen to suggest the "naughtiness" of the popular yellowbacks, but its content was of much higher quality. It featured such writers as Arnold Bennett, Henry James, and Oscar

Wilde, and drawings by Aubrey Beardsley and Max Beerbohm.

Both yellowbacks and *The Yellow Book* belong to the past. Today we have only the *yellow pages*, the classified telephone directory listing subscribers by the products and services they offer, usually printed on yellow paper and often bound with a yellow cover as well. Actually, the *OED* cites a Sears, Roebuck catalog from 1908 that said, "See the yellow pages at the back of the book," referring to the index, printed on yellow paper. But the familiar telephone yellow pages have been so called only since about 1950. Sometimes the term is transferred to other classified directories as well.

❧ *Yellow for Caution* ❧

A *yellow traffic light*, often called *amber* rather than yellow, means to proceed with caution. It usually precedes a red light, which means stop at once. This term has been around since 1960 or so.

Similarly, a *yellow line* painted along a curb indicates that cars are not permitted to wait in that area, and/or parking there is forbidden. A solid yellow line down the center of the road means that traffic is to stay on one side of it, without crossing to pass another car. Sometimes this is indicated by a double yellow line.

A *yellow alert* signifies an initial state of readiness for an emergency, either in defense against an enemy or some other kind of emergency (a nuclear accident, for example). This term dates from the mid-1960s.

None of these has anything to do with the *yellow brick road* that Dorothy is told to follow in *The Wizard of Oz*. Indeed, *Follow the Yellow Brick Road*, to discover ultimate truth, is the title of a song from the motion picture (1939), with lyrics by E. Y. Harburg. In 1979 the actor Ray Bolger, who played the Scarecrow in the movie, spoke at the funeral of Jack Haley, who played the Tin Man, and said, "How lonely it is going to be now on the Yellow Brick Road."

&ce; *She Wore a Yellow Ribbon* &ce;

"They're everywhere," wrote Patti Doten in the *Boston Globe* on February 9, 1991. "From Boston to the Berkshires, yellow ribbons adorn houses and fences, lapels and car antennas, buildings and trees, bridges and elementary schools, baby carriages and flagpoles."

The message of this outburst of *yellow-ribbon* decoration was support for U.S. troops who were at that time engaged in fighting against Iraq in the Persian Gulf War. No one is exactly sure where the custom originated. In this century it was used in the 1970s by the families of soldiers returning from the controversial Vietnam War, who hung yellow ribbons on trees. It was about this time, in 1973, that Tony Orlando's song, *Tie a Yellow Ribbon 'Round the Old Oak Tree,* became popular, but the song, about a Georgia woman who tied a hundred ribbons on a white oak tree to welcome her sweetheart home from prison, had nothing to do with veterans.

Another source suggested is the Civil War, when Union cavalry uniforms were dark blue with yellow kerchiefs. When a soldier went off to fight, he would leave the kerchief with his wife or sweetheart as a remembrance.

Still another possible source is a song in Oscar Brand's 1923 collection *Bawdy Songs and Back-Room Ballads.* Sung to an old tune, it goes, "Around her neck she wore a yellow ribbon, she wore it for her lover who was far, far away." One version substitutes "sailor" for "lover" and another has it "yaller" ribbon, but the idea is the same.

Whatever the ultimate origin, the yellow ribbon symbolizes remembrance, which is far more positive than most of the feelings this color is identified with.

Index

Terms are arranged in alphabetical order, letter by letter, up to the comma in cases of inversion. If a comma is part of the main term (as in *red, white, and blue*), the term is alphabetized as though there were no comma; if a comma is not part of the term (as in *red, symbolism of*), alphabetization stops at the comma. Cross-references to another term in the index are indicated by small capital letters, such as *see* BLACK AS.